Clesham, editor

REGISTER OF THE PARISH OF ST NICHOLAS, GALWAY

THE REGISTER

OF THE

PARISH OF

ST NICHOLAS, GALWAY

1792-1840

Edited by

Brigid Clesham

REPRESENTATIVE CHURCH BODY LIBRARY,
DUBLIN

Typeset at the Representative Church Body Library by Pam Stanley

Published by the
Representative Church Body Library
Braemor Park, Dublin 14, Ireland

© Representative Church Body 2004

All rights reserved. No part of this publication
may be copied, reproduced or transmitted in any
form or by any means, without permission
of the publisher

ISBN 0-9523000-9-5

Printed by
Colour Books, Dublin, Ireland

Contents

Preface	7
Introduction	9
Abbreviations	23
Register of St Nicholas, Galway	24
Appendix A: A list of regiments of the British Army and Militia stationed in Galway, 1792-1840	144
Appendix B: Biographical notes on the clergy of the parish of St Nicholas, Galway, 1792-1840	145
Bibliography	152
Index	154

Preface

This is the ninth volume in the Representative Church Body Library's parish register series and the first to deal with a parish in the west of Ireland. I am grateful to Brigid Clesham for drawing my attention to this unintentional lacuna.

Like its predecessors this volume seeks to make accessible to a wider readership primary source material for historical and genealogical research and to draw attention to the resources in the RCB Library which is, *inter alia*, the Church of Ireland's principal repository for its archives and manuscripts. It is also hoped that the publication will contribute to the conservation of the register by reducing the number of occasions on which it needs to be consulted.

The register of Galway, the parish of the principal city of Connacht, and the largest Church of Ireland parish, in terms of population, in the diocese and province of Tuam, was an obvious volume to prepare for publication. Its contents echo the role of the city as a civil and ecclesiastical administrative centre, a sea port, a garrison and much else and are, to some extent, a reflection of that strange combination of remoteness and sophistication which has made Galway seem exciting and exotic to those who dwell on the east coast of Ireland.

I am grateful to Brigid Clesham for agreeing to edit the register and for bringing to the task the forensic skills of the archivist, an instinctive understanding of much of the context which comes readily to a daughter of the rectory and the familiarity of many years of residence in the locality. I am indebted to the Church of Ireland Publications Officer, Susan Hood, for her patient and invaluable work an in-house editor, to Pam Stanley for her typesetting skills and to the Head of Communications and Synod Services, Janet Maxwell for her support.

Raymond Refaussé
Series Editor

Introduction

The earliest register for the Church of Ireland parish of St Nicholas, Galway dates from 1792. It contains a fairly complete run of marriages from that year until 1839, baptisms from 1800 to 1840 together with a less complete run of burials for the period 1832-1838 and some earlier odd entries of burial between 1800 and 1820. Of the 1360 entries, only a few are repeated, and the complete content may be broken down as follows: 910 baptisms, 410 marriages and 40 burials. Successive clergy of the parish kept the register in local custody until 1995, when it was transferred to the Representative Church Body Library, Dublin, which is the principal repository of Church of Ireland records.[1] Two contemporary sources, Hardiman's *History of the town and county of the town of Galway* (1820) and Lewis's *Topographical dictionary of Ireland* (1837), as well as more recent publications, have been used to give a background introduction to this work.

Galway at the beginning of the nineteenth century

A corporation created by a charter of Charles II, dated 1677, governed the town of Galway. The corporation consisted of a mayor, two sheriffs, a number of burgesses, a recorder, town clerk, constables of the staple, sword bearer, chamberlain, water-bailiff and other officers. The corporation sent two members to Parliament until the Act of Union, which came into effect in 1801, when its representation was reduced to one member.

Galway was unique in Ireland in that a two-mile radius centred on Fort Hill, had been constituted a distinct county by a charter early in the reign of James I. This area became known as the county of the town of Galway under the charter of 1677, and was enlarged in the late eighteenth century to comprise approximately 23,000 statute acres consisting of the parish of St Nicholas, most of the parish of Rahoon, and part of the parish of Oranmore. All local government and judicial matters were administered by a grand jury. In 1820, Hardiman estimated that the population of both town and county of the town was about 40,000. By 1824, a provincial directory (based on figures from

---

[1] RCB Library, P.519/1/1.

the 1821 census) estimated that while 27,827 comprised the population of the town proper, if the liberties were included a total figure in excess 40,000 would be reached.[2]

Until the early eighteenth century, Galway was a busy maritime port, trading mainly in wine and provisions. A flourishing trade was made possible by the close familial ties of several catholic merchants in the town who had relatives in France and Spain, allowing a continental trading network to develop. The corporation, which was responsible for the regulation of trade, was in the hands of a small protestant group, who, anxious to control its affairs for their own ends, showed little initiative and constantly quarrelled among themselves. Restrictions on catholics brought about by the penal laws made it difficult to conduct business and as a result, trade had diminished by the mid-eighteenth century. Smuggling flourished, the harbour suffered neglect, and only following a sustained flow of petitions from merchants were the ruinous quays finally repaired in the 1790s. In spite of these restrictions and especially with the relaxation of the penal laws, trade took off again, which resulted in some revival in its fortunes as a regional capital towards the end of the century.[3]

When the register begins, in 1792, it is representative of a prospering urban centre, influenced by a wide diversity of cultural and geographical factors. Many of these influences stemmed from Galway's role as a seaport. Galway merchants traded with the New World and some kept their contacts in Spain and France and other European countries. Galway ships were also visiting developing markets in the Far East. Persons from locations as diverse as Trinidad, New England, Bordeaux and Stockholm, as well as various parts of England, Scotland and Wales, are all mentioned in the register between 1792 and 1840, capturing the town's international culture. In 1828 miners from the English counties of Cornwall and Derbyshire were working in the lead mines at Tully, just outside Galway.[4]

---

[2] James Hardiman, *The history of the town and county of the town of Galway*, (revised edition, Galway, 1985), p. 284; J. Pigot, *City of Dublin and Hibernian provincial directory* (Dublin, 1824).
[3] J.G. Simms, 'Connacht in the eighteenth century', in *Irish Historical Studies*, xi, 42, Sept 1958, pp. 124-5.
[4] See pp. 77-8 of the register.

Visiting sailors and the many soldiers quartered in Galway also gave the town's population a mobile and cosmopolitan dimension, and again this is captured in the St Nicholas's register. Members of the crew of brigs, sloops and a type of ship known as an 'East Indiaman' are all recorded. Hardiman writes that the year 1794 was 'rendered remarkable for the arrival of the homeward bound East India fleet',[5] which included the *Minerva,* a ship constructed in the port of Galway for Messrs Walter and John Burke in 1791.[6] Marriage entries for two members of the crew of the *Minerva* are recorded in 1794 and 1796.[7] Between the years 1824 and 1827 there are four entries in the register relating to crew members of a brig of war named the *Plumper.*[8]

Other signs of improvement revealed during the early years of the nineteenth century include the expansion of the town beyond the old town walls, which had been levelled in many places to make way for the erection of new buildings. The west suburbs became a distinct location, situated to the west and south west of the Claddagh village.[9] The east suburbs extended beyond Meyrick Square, later known as Eyre Square, to the east and south east, and it was in this area that the new Erasmus Smith school was built in 1815 at a cost of £8,000. This school was generally known as 'the College'. Evidence from the register also reveals strong links between the college and the parish of St Nicholas. The Revd Drelingcourt Young Campbell was appointed master of the college in 1768. He was the first cleric to make entries in the register, in his additional capacity as one of the vicars of Galway. Another master of the college, the Revd John Whitley (who served in this role between 1815 and 1837) was also chaplain to the military garrison in the town, and performed many of the ceremonies relating to soldiers recorded in the register.

---

[5] Hardiman, *The history of the town and county,* p. 190. The marriages of three crew members from these ships were recorded in August 1794 (see p. 3 of the register).

[6] P. O'Dowd, *Galway city* (Galway, 1998), p. 46. See also G.A. Hayes McCoy, 'Three Galway ships', in *JGAGS,* xxviii, pp. 1-4, which refers to the building of the *Minerva* and her maiden voyage to the United States in May 1792.

[7] See pp. 3 & 5 of the register.

[8] See pp. 51, 58, 61 & 63 of the register.

[9] O'Dowd, *Galway city,* p. 24, in which Michael Logan's map of Galway, dated 1818, is reproduced from James Hardiman's book of 1820.

By the beginning of the nineteenth century, the main exports of the town were corn, kelp and marble, and the main imports were timber and iron. Flour milling had, by this time, taken over as the principal industry. Power generated by the many waterways in the town enabled the development of other industries, such as brewing, distilling and paper manufacturing. The register shows that two paper manufacturers, Reuben Hughes and James Francis, resided in the parish in the first decade of the nineteenth century, and there is a reference to the 'West Paper Mills' in 1835.[10] The river and sea also contributed to the economy of the town by the provision of a lucrative salmon fishery and a great supply of many varieties of fish from the bay. The fishermen of the Claddagh largely controlled the sea fishing. Six officers and 51 men constituted the coast guard of the district, who had their main station in Galway, with subordinate stations at Ballyvaughan, Kilcolgan, Barna, Cashel Bay, Aran Islands, Fairhill and Kilkerran.[11] The children of some 14 members of the coast guard and water guard were baptised in St Nicholas's between 1828 and 1837.

The town was enhanced by the erection of new buildings, such as the town and county gaols, both begun about 1810, a courthouse in 1815, the Pro-cathedral in 1816 and the Salmon Weir Bridge in 1818. Alexander Nimmo designed a new pier at Mutton Island and made plans for the construction of new docks. The child of a stonemason, employed in the building of the lighthouse at Mutton Island, was baptised in 1816.[12] The building of docks, quays and a canal was supervised by some of the more prominent merchants of the town who formed themselves into a chamber of commerce. The opening of branches of the various national banks followed these developments.[13] Urban expansion and industrial development during the early nineteenth century are also reflected in the register by the wide range of occupations recorded for the men of the parish of St Nicholas.

---

[10] See p. 141 of the register.
[11] Samuel Lewis, *Topographical dictionary of Ireland* (London, 1837), vol. 1, p. 647.
[12] See p. 23 of the register.
[13] *Slater's Directory* (London, 1856) states that there were branches of three national banks in the town.

Besides the military and maritime occupations recorded, many men in the parish were employed as tradesmen such as nailers, rope makers, cabinet makers, shoemakers and bakers. As the nineteenth century progressed, evidence of the town's expansion and the control of seafaring operations becoming subject to tighter regulations is made clear by the increase of official occupations such as tidewaiters, customs or excise men, policemen, recorded in the register. The register also captures the presence of comedians, musicians, dancing masters and booksellers in the town during the early decades of the nineteenth century – a measure of the extensive cultural interests of the local population. Senior officials of the town and county administration feature too, including persons such as John Kearney, comptroller of customs, and John Fitzsimons, governor of the county gaol, both of whom had their children baptised in St Nicholas's parish church.

A few old Galway tribe and gentry family names appear also, including members of the Blakes of Menlough, the Lamberts of Castle Ellen, and the Brownes of Moyne. Commerical development brought newcomers to the town, such as Charles Copeland, manager of the Provincial Bank by 1832, and Charles Trounselle, who had a position of prominence at the Newcastle distillery from at least 1831.[14] Other noteworthy parishioners included 'Mr Logan the surveyor', whose son John was baptised in 1826.[15]

The military presence in the town

One recent analysis of the British Army influence in Galway concludes that it 'formed a prominent part of the population of Galway in the nineteenth century, and played a major role in city life'.[16] Besides their official role, the soldiers made an important contribution to the social life of the town. Officers attended functions

---

[14] See pp. 95, 143, & 144 of the register.
[15] See p. 64 of the register. Logan produced a survey map of Galway in 1818, see John Andrews, *Plantation acres: an historical study of the Irish land surveyor and his maps* (Belfast, 1985), p. 345.
[16] Anne M.A. Mannion, *The social geography of the British Army in nineteenth-century Ireland with specific reference to Galway* (unpublished MA thesis, U.C.G., 1994), p. 85.

such as the theatre, dances, shooting parties, and all ranks generally interacted with the town community, including marriage with local girls. There were three barracks for foot soldiers, namely the Castle barrack, the Shambles barrack and the Lombard Street barrack in which 900 men could be accommodated in the 1820s. Before the disturbances of 1798, some of the inhabitants of Galway had formed themselves into eight companies of volunteers to preserve the peace of the town. At this time they were under the command of General Hutchinson, who on hearing of the French landing at Killala, went to join General Lake with the garrison and yeomanry of the town and shared in Lake's defeat at the 'Races of Castlebar'.[17]

Many different regiments of foot and militia were stationed in the town during the period covered by the register. The militia regiments were raised from the civilian population on a county by county basis, to supplement the regular army at times of unrest. When peace was restored they were disbanded. A list of regiments stationed in Galway between 1792 and 1840 is provided in this volume in appendix A. The absence of a battalion in the town after 1815 captures the sense of relative peace that prevailed in Ireland following the Battle of Waterloo. Instead of battalions of militia, only the regular army was stationed in Galway to maintain law and order during this time of peace. Gradually, as the century progressed, this latter role was taken over by the police - a development captured in St Nicholas's register in 1822, when the son of Anthony Saver 'of the Police Establishment' was baptised.[18] Several other entries concerning policemen and their families follow, and in 1826 reference is made to a police station at Oranmore, and to others at Tully in 1830 and at Oughterard in 1836.[19]

The register records both marriages between soldiers and local girls and the baptisms of children of members of the many regiments stationed in Galway between 1792 and 1840. Out of the 130 marriages conducted in St Nicholas's between 1792 and 1806, no less

---

[17] This was John Hutchinson, later Lord Hutchinson and 2nd Earl of Donoughmore. One of General Hutchinson's servants and his brother Lorenzo were married in St Nicholas church in 1798, (see p. 7 of the register).
[18] See p. 42 of the register.
[19] See pp. 42, 64, 108 & 144 of the register.

than 53 bridegrooms were soldiers. The prevailing presence of the 30th Regiment of Foot in the parish is captured by the baptisms of 14 children of soldiers in that regiment, between October 1833 and May 1834. The transient nature of each regiment's stay in Galway is reflected in the fact that very few soldiers had more than one child baptised while stationed in Galway. This was to change in the later decades of the century, when regiments began to be stationed in Galway for longer periods of time.[20] The registers of the Roman Catholic, Presbyterian and Methodist churches in Galway also provide evidence of the strength of the military presence in the town.[21]

The parish of St Nicholas, Galway

The parish of St Nicholas comprised 3,046 statute acres and was part of the wardenship of Galway. The wardenship was an unusual arrangement, originally instituted in 1484, whereby a college of a warden and eight vicars was appointed by the mayor and corporation to administer the parish of St Nicholas, independent of episcopal control. From the time of the Reformation, a catholic and a protestant wardenship operated along side each other. In 1820, Hardiman listed the possessions of the protestant warden as follows – the vicarage of the town, with the rectories and vicarages of Ballinacourty, Clare Galway, Kilcummin, Moycullen, Oranmore, Rahoon and Shruel. It had been endowed with the dissolved monasteries of Annaghdown and Ballintubber in the reign of Elizabeth I. Hardiman estimated that the annual income of the warden was approximately £1,000, out of which various expenses had to be paid, including a yearly stipend of £75 per annum to each of the two vicars. Although the warden was to be elected every year, it appears that by the nineteenth century this was a formality and the incumbent continued in his post for successive years. An unsuccessful challenge to the Revd James Daly's position as warden in August 1815 is recorded in the Galway Corporation records.[22] The wardenship was officially abolished in 1841 under the Irish Municipal Regulations Act, although the Revd James Daly continued to hold the title until his death in 1864. Although there had

---

[20] Mannion, *Social geography*, p. 104.
[21] ibid.
[22] Galway Corporation Records Liber K1, James Hardiman Library Archives, N.U.I.G.

originally been eight vicars, this number was reduced, but at what time or under whose authority, is not recorded in extant parish records.[23]

The church of St Nicholas is a cruciform structure, dedicated to St Nicholas (the original Santa Claus and Archbishop of Myra – an important seaport in Asia Minor). It was originally built as a small parish church in 1320, in the centre of the Norman town. Various alterations and additions were made, most notably in the sixteenth century by the enlargement of the northern and southern aisles under the patronage of the French and Lynch families respectively. The church is noted for the coats of arms and embellished tombs of members of the various Galway tribes, and is generally considered to be the largest medieval parish church in Ireland. One historian describes it as follows:-

> Irish gothic with Renaissance influences, but its details, as a result of its history vary considerably in style. Built of hard, blue-grey limestone, the interior effects especially are imposing and beautiful, and from every point of view the church is a remarkable and interesting building, a splendid example of the local school of masonry.[24]

Some of the nineteenth-century structural changes made to the building are recorded in the earliest vestry minute book for the parish of St Nicholas, which dates from 1805 and remains in local custody. The vestry minutes are largely concerned with the appointment of parochial officers and apploters (responsible for surveying property for the tithe applotment), the approval of parish accounts, the inspection of parish children and the allocation of pews but also allude to building. For example, a vestry meeting was called on 23rd May

---

[23] J. Fleetwood Berry, *The story of St Nicholas' collegiate church, Galway* (Galway, 1912), pp. 42-6. Hardiman (1820) stated that the Revd James Daly, warden, who was resident in the town, had the care of all the parishes of the wardenship, and further stated that duty was performed by him and two resident vicars, Hardiman, *The history of the town and county,* p. 250. Pigot's Directory (1824) and Slater's Directory (1856) as well as Leslie's succession list for Tuam, all record there being four vicars for Galway during the nineteenth century.
[24] M. D. O'Sullivan, *Old Galway* (Cambridge, 1942), p. 450.

1820, for the purpose of 'making the church more commodious to the congregation than it is at present'.[25] Alterations to the church commenced as a result of this meeting. They continued over the next two decades, and together with the increase in the number of baptisms and marriages recorded in the register, indicate a growing protestant population in the town in the period after the Napoleonic Wars.

The register

The register measures 27x38x7½ centimeters. It has a dark brown leather cover, which originally encased two backing boards at each end. The front backing board is now missing and part of the cover has been torn. The cover has come away from the pages of the register, which are still loosely sewn together. The volume includes three detached sheets, two of which contain burial and baptismal entries. The lack of the front backing board has caused a large amount of wear to what is now the first page of the register, much of which is faded, difficult to read and in some parts completely missing. Some entries are only decipherable under ultra violent light. In the published text the phrase [text lost] indicates where part of the page of the register is missing. Usually this involves the loss of no more than one or two words in each case.

The register contains approximately 908 records of baptisms from 1800-1837, with one baptism for each of the years 1839-1840; approximately 410 marriage entries for the years 1792-1837, with one marriage recorded in 1839; and approximately 39 burials recorded in the years 1800, 1802, 1803, 1818, 1820, 1832, 1834 and 1836-1838. One unfortunate family, the Lydons, buried four members between 11 April and 23 June 1837, most likely the victims of cholera.[26] The ratio of burials to baptisms is very small and it is obvious that the deaths of only a few parishioners are recorded, reflecting perhaps the emphasis on the living rather than the dead, and the significance of holy baptism. Nevertheless the entries provide a graphic account of the nature of the protestant population of Galway in the early decades of the nineteenth century, in particular the involvement of many parishioners in military, official and maritime occupations.

---

[25] Vestry minute book of St Nicholas's Galway, 1805-1910.
[26] See p. 440 of the register.

With a few stray exceptions, the first part of the register runs in a chronological sequence from 1792 up to 1834 (on page 99). After this, the sequence (from page 100) reverts to the year 1812 with a jump to the year 1823 (on page 102), and thereafter various sequences cover the years between 1812 and 1838 (to page 442) when the main part of the register ends.

In its present binding, the register is preceded by a 70-page index which was originally at the back of the volume. For some reason, the Revd John Campbell kept the record of baptisms in the front pages of the index, from May 1800 (and possibly earlier, as pages may have been lost) until January 1808. From February 1808 the recording of baptisms continued on page 15 in the main part of the register. Other entries of baptisms, marriages and burials were made intermittently by various clergy in the index rather than the register proper. For example under the letter 'F', the funeral and burial of Catherine Strogen is recorded as having taken place on 15 June 1800, as is the conversion of Michael Flahertie on 4 March 1810, but these two entries are not repeated elsewhere in the volume.

Apart from these idiosyncrasies, the pages of the index have also been used for their proper function and there is a fairly comprehensive index to the names of the persons in the register, with the exception of the additional baptismal entries made in the index pages and many of the brides' names in the marriage entries throughout the register. It is apparent that names were entered in the index at the same time as the entry was made in the register and although there are some inconsistencies, the index has been helpful in confirming the spelling of particular surnames. In one or two instances, the index provides additional information for the entry to which it relates. Such additional information has been included in footnotes or in the body of the published text. The page numbering of the published text corresponds with the original numbering in ink of the pages of the register.

Throughout the register proper, and in the index and loose pages, it is evident that on some occasions an entry was made on a blank page, which may at a later stage have been filled up with entries for other years. Occasionally an entry appears twice. Some pages were cut out of the volume; these include pages 153-4 on which at least some entries were recorded as the pages are listed in the index.

In the published text of the register, the spelling has been left as was the practice in the original register. However capitals and punctuation have, to some extent, been standardized. Square brackets have been used where there is some uncertainty as to the exact text, and for editorial remarks. Occasionally there is a blank space in an entry. This generally occurs where the christian name of the father or mother of the child being baptised is missing. Sometimes the space for the name of a witness to a marriage is left blank. In the published text a blank space is indicated by the word [blank].

The names of witnesses to marriages were included in the register from 1818 and were sometimes preceded by the word 'Present'. John Steadman, parish clerk during the 1820s, was the most frequent witness to parochial marriages, while other witnesses included Henry Caddy (sexton), Henry Manning (parish clerk in the 1830s), and Andrew Reed and his son John (who served consecutively as churchwardens between 1816 and 1827). The names of witnesses have been put on a separate line in the published text, in accordance with the format of most cases in the register.

From 1792 and until 1820, the register appears to have been fairly consistently kept by the Revd Drelincourt Young Campbell, followed by his son, the Revd John Campbell (for detailed biographical information, see appendix B at the end of this volume). Campbell senior, as master of the Erasmus Smith school and vicar of Galway, appears to have conducted and recorded all marriages in the parish between April 1792 and February 1799. He died on 5 August 1799. His son, John Campbell, became one of the vicars of Galway in that year, and continued to keep the register commenced by his father some seven years before. Campbell junior died on 13 March 1818, aged 46. The phrase 'dying write I this' written in his own hand (found at the end of page 26 of the register) indicates his awareness of imminent death. His name does not appear in the register after February 1818, and the keeping of the register from then on appears to have becomes more dependent on the diligence of other members of the parish clergy, who either made the entries themselves or, increasingly depended on the services of the parish clerks, John Steadman and Henry Manning.

It is not clear whether or not the baptisms and marriages performed and recorded by the Campbells and the Revd Robert Shaw in the years 1792-1817 were the only ones that took place in the parish but they are the only ones recorded. There was certainly a rise in the number of baptisms and marriages entered in the register after 1820. The annual average for the years 1810-19 was 19 baptisms, with an increase to 28 baptisms for the years 1820-29. However the highest number of baptisms was recorded in 1805 with a total of 40. The baptisms recorded after 1818 often give the christian name of the mother of the child, and occasionally her maiden name which provides useful supplementary genealogical information. From the mid- 1820s, the date of birth of the child, in addition to the baptismal date, began to be kept.

The baptisms of a number of foundlings are included in the register between 1805 and 1822,[27] and an entry on one of the loose pages indicates that one foundling arrived with a label attached to instruct how the child was to be named.[28] At the other end of the social scale, the Revd John D'Arcy privately baptised a few children of the local gentry in their own homes.[29] Other evidence of this mobile service is found at Oranmore where a number of children of the police constabulary were baptised at the police barracks.[30]

---

[27] See pp. 21, 23, 25, 36, 39, 41, (2), (6), (10) & (11) of the register.
[28] See p. 10 of the register.
[29] See pp. 77, 162 & 170 of the register.
[30] See pp. 53, 61, 64 & 102 of the register.

The gravestone of the Revd James Daly records that he was warden of Galway between 1811 and 1864. He succeeded his father, the Revd Ralph Daly, who, although he served as warden from 1786 to 1810, does not feature in the register as all. From 1818 the Revd James Daly and the Revd Edward Bourke appear to have kept the register between them, while from 1820 onwards they were additionally assisted by the Revds Henry Morgan, John D'Arcy and John Whitley (for detailed biographies, see appendix B). Whitley was the master of the Erasmus Smith Grammar School (the college) and also held the position of garrison chaplain from 1818. The baptisms of his six children between the years 1819 and 1833 are all recorded together.[31] The Revd Henry Morgan, vicar of Galway between 1821 and 1840, often performed ceremonies on behalf of the Revd John Whitley. Morgan appears to have been fairly meticulous about his entries in the register, in marked contrast to his contemporary the Revd John D'Arcy, who, on occasions made very brief entries. Notwithstanding his tendancy to be scanty with the pen, D'Arcy became a venerated person in Galway on account of his instigation and implementation of many building improvements in the town.[32] He was vicar of Galway from 1821-1864 and subsequently became rector from 1864-72. The Revd Edward Eyre Maunsell of Fort Eyre, county Galway, became a vicar of Galway in the early 1830s. It is apparent however that he had been active in the parish much earlier as he is recorded as one of the churchwardens in 1815.[33] It was Maunsell to whom genealogists can be particularly grateful, as he commenced the practice of recording the maiden name of mothers as well as the child's name, in some of his baptismal entries.

Kirwan's charity

In the register there are a number of references to Kirwan's charity including accounts of the distribution of the interest from the investment of this bequest in various years. Hardiman writes that a Mr Kirwan of London vested a sum of money in trustees for the

---

[31] See p. 27 of the register.
[32] Higgins and Heringklee, *Monuments of St Nicholas collegiate church*, p. 7.
[33] Galway vestry minute book, St Nicholas collegiate church, Galway, 1805-1910, p. 180.

benefit of 'distressed individuals of the Galway names'.[34] Lewis records that Mr Kirwan left the interest of £500 to the warden of Galway, in trust for the benefit of the protestant poor. The register records that the Kirwan bequest was invested in new government four per cent stock by 1823, and in the Galway Savings Bank by 1827. The distribution of the half-yearly interest of this bequest is recorded on pages 287-292 of the register for the years 1822, 1823, 1825, 1827, 1831 and 1832. The distribution of the interest from another bequest - that of Mrs Halliday - is also mentioned on one of the register's index pages.[35]

---

[34] Hardiman *The history of the town and county,* p. 307.
[35] See p. (5) of the register.

General abbreviations

Abh/Abishop = Archbishop
Adj./Adjutnt = adjutant
A.M. = Master of Arts
Apl/Apr. = April
assistt = assistant
Augt/Aug. = August
atty = attorney
bapd = baptized
Batt./Batn/Battn/Bn = Battalion
BLGI = Burkes Landed Gentry of Ireland
Bt/Bart = Baronet
burd. = buried
Captn = Captain
Ch. = Church
Ch. Off. = Chief Officer
Co. = County
Col = Colonel
C.W.s = Churchwardens
D.D. = Doctor of Divinity
decd = deceased
Decemr/Decr = December
Dio. = Diocese
Do = ditto
Dr = Doctor
Esqr or Esq. = Esquire
Febr./Feb./F./Feby = February
G.C./Gn Ch./Garn Chapn = Garrison Chaplain
Govr = Governor
Honble = Honourable
Infy = Infantry
inst = instant
Jan./Jany = January
JGAHS = Journal of the Galway Archaeological and Historical Society
Jun. or Junr = Junior
Lieut/Lt = Lieutenant
Mt = Mount
Novr/Novembr/ Nov. = November
N.U.I.G. = National University of Ireland, Galway
Oct./Octr = October
RCB = Representative Church Body
Regimt/Rgt/Regt = Regiment
R.E.= Royal Engineers
Rev./Revd = Reverend
R.N. = Royal Navy
sd = said
Sen. = Senior
Septem./Sept./ Sepr = September
Sergt = Sergeant
Sr = Sir

Christian name abbreviations

Alexr = Alexander
Andw = Andrew
Anth. = Anthony
Benjn/Benj. = Benjamin
Cathne = Catherine
Chas = Charles
Const.=[Constance/Constantine]
Danl = Daniel
Edw./Edwd = Edward
Elizth = Elizabeth
Frans = Francis
Geo. = George
Jas = James
Jno. = John
Margt = Margaret
Matt. = Matthew
Michl = Michael
Nathl = Nathaniel
Patk = Patrick
Rich./Richd = Richard
Rob./Robt = Robert
Thos/Tho. = Thomas
Wm/Willm = William

T.C.D. = Trinity College Dublin
U.C.G. = University College Galway
Vet./Vett./Vetn = Veteran
Vicr = Vicar

[Page] 1

Arthur Thomas of Ardnesallagh in the Parish of Kilcummin, married to Elinor Cottingham of the same place, on the 28th day of April 1792, D.Y. Campbell, Vicar

Stephen Bartholomew Blake of Summerville Esqr, married to Margaret D'Arcy of Wellpark, widow, on the 20th day of May 1792, D.Y. Campbell, Vicar

John Tvey, soldier of the 56th Regt, married to Margaret Dunn of the town of Galway, the 25th day of June 1792, D.Y. Campbell, Vicar

David Standford of Ballinderry in the County of Galway, married to Ellis Burke of Oranmore, spinster, the 24th day of July 1792, D.Y. Campbell, Vicar

Thomas Parker O Flaherty of Milesian Hall in the County of Galway, Esqr, married to Maria Burke of Derrymacloughney in sd county, the 19th day of September 1792, D.Y. Campbell, Vicar

Luke Jaques, soldier in the 27th Regt of Foot, married to Rose Hedrington of the town Galway, but lately of Ireconnaught, the 29th day of January 1792, by Revd Robert Shawe

Thomas Browne Junr of Galway Esqr, married to Mary Jones of Galway, spinster, the 27th day of October 1792, D.Y. Campbell, Vicar

Martin French Lynch, Counsellor at Law, Esqr of the town of Galway, married to Jane Eyre, widow, the 29th day of October 1792, D.Y. Campbell, Vicar

Henry Horsefall, ensign in the 39th Regt of Foot, married to Jane Lewin, spinster, the 31st day of October 1792, D.Y. Campbell, Vicar

John Davidson, soldier of the 39th Regt of Foot, married to Mary Holliday, spinster, the 6th day of November 1792, D.Y. Campbell, Vicar

John Doyle, apothecary and surgeon, married to Celia Field, spinster, the 12th day of November 1792, D.Y. Campbell, Vicar

[Page] 2

John Campbell, soldier in the 39th Regt of Foot then quartered in Galway, married to Anne Browne, spinster of sd town, on the 27th day of December 1792, D.Y. Campbell, Vicar

William Purdie, Lieutenant in the 39th Regt of Foot then quartered in Galway, married Margaret Mannen, spinster, daughter of Mr Timothy

Mannen of sd town, on the 27th day of April 1793 three, D.Y. Campbell, Vicar

Edmund FitzPatrick Esqr married to Hellen Burke, spinster, daughter of Robert Burke of Gortnomona Esqr, on the 1st day of August 1793 three, D.Y. Campbell, Vicar

William Phillips lately of Corofin in the County of Clare, dancing master, married to Elizabeth Martin, spinster, daughter of Thomas Martin Esqr lately deceased, on the 21st day of August 1793 three, D.Y. Campbell, Vicar

Garrett Clinch lately of Dublin, servant of Thos Kelly atty, married to Bridget O Laughlin, lately of Loughrea, spinster, on the 29th day of August 1793 three, D.Y. Campbell, Vicar

John Driver of the ship *Sarah*, mariner, married to Bridget Sheridan of the town of Galway, spinster on the 1st day of September 1793 three, D.Y. Campbell, Vicar

Walter Blake of Somerville Esqr, son of S[i]r Walter Blake Baronet, married to Letitia Bingham, widow and relict of the late Henry Bingham of Newbrook Esqr, on the 21st day of February 1794 four, D.Y. Campbell, Vicar

[Page] 3

William Hedger, of the *Minerva* East Indiaman, married to Jane Hart of the Woodquay, Galway, spinster, on the 6th day of August 1794 four, D.Y. Campbell, Vicar

William Shepherd, mail coach driver, married to Mary FitzPatrick of the town of Galway, spinster, on the 6th day of August 1794 four, D.Y. Campbell, Vicar

George Cheverson, mariner, married to Margaret Hanna alias Wheeler, widow of the town of Galway, on the 6th day of August 1794 four, D.Y. Campbell, Vicar

William Tweedy, one of the mates of the *Earl of Cornwallis* East Indiaman, married to Jane Maria Deane of the town of Galway, spinster, on the 7th day of August 1794 four, D.Y. Campbell, Vicar

James McCabe, of the *Earl of Chesterfield* East Indiaman, married to Margaret Barry alias Joyes, of the town of Galway, widow, on the 7th day of August 1794 four, D.Y. Campbell, Vicar

John Flannery of the Parish of Donoughpatrick, married to Mary Malley of the same spinster, on the 11th day of August 1794 four, D.Y. Campbell, Vicar

Patrick Davin of the Parish of Killcummin, married to Letty Hanbury of the same Parish, on the 17th day of August 1794 four, D.Y. Campbell, Vicar

[Page] 4

David Devereux Wray, one of the company of comedians, married to Mary Lynch, one of the sd company, spinster, on the 31st day of August 1794 four, D.Y. Campbell, Vicar

Thomas Naghten of Thomastown in the County of Roscommon Esqr, married to Miss Anne D'Arcy of Wellpark near Galway, on the 25th day of September 1794 four, D.Y. Campbell, Vicar

Francis McDonald, soldier in the Royal Tyrone Regiment of Militia, married to Bridget Kiggins of Galway, on the 30th day of December 1794 four, D.Y. Campbell, Vicar

Michael Daly, soldier in the Royal Tyrone Regiment of Militia, married to Mary Kelly of Galway, on the 4th day of January 1795 five, D.Y. Campbell, Vicar

Edward Develin, soldier in the Royal Tyrone Regiment of Militia, married to Mary Flyn of Galway, on the 9th day of February 1795 five, D.Y. Campbell, Vicar

Bartholomew Tierney, coachmaker to the mailcoach, married to Elinor Eaton of Galway, daughter of Mr Eaton one of the tide waiters, on the 26th day of May 1795 five, D.Y. Campbell, Vicar

John Lackey of the town of Galway ropemaker, married to Mary Hicks of sd town, spinster, on the 7th day of June 1795 five, D.Y. Campbell, Vicar

Joseph Carter, musician in the Royal Tyrone Regt of Militia, married to Anne Cahil of the town of Galway, spinster, on the 15th day of June 1795 five, D.Y. Campbell, Vicar

Charles Malim Esqr, Captain in the Northampton Regt of Fencibles, married to Miss Catherine Deane of the town of Galway, on the 12th day of July 1795 five, D.Y. Campbell, Vicar

[Page] 5

William Walsh, mariner commander of the sloop *Joe* of Liverpool, married to Miss Jane Squibb of Galway, on the 13th day of January 1796 six, D.Y. Campbell, Vicar

James Kennedy, shoemaker, married to Catherine Cox of Galway, spinster, on the 28th day of January 1796 six, D.Y. Campbell, Vicar

John Delano, commander of the brig *Polly* of New Bedford in New England now lying in the harbour of Galway, married to Mary Dolan, of the town of Galway, spinster, on the 11th day of June 1796 six, D.Y. Campbell, Vicar

Ulick O'Brien of the town of Galway Esqr, married to Louisa Bingham, spinster, daughter of the late Henry Bingham of Newbrook Esqr, on the 7th day of September 1796 six, D.Y. Campbell, Vicar

Francis David Kirwan of the town of Galway, lately of Bourdeaux Esqr, married publicly to Margaret Blake of Drum (they having been before clandestinely marry'd), on the 18th day of October 1796 six, D.Y. Campbell, Vicar

John Johnson of the ship *Minerva* of Galway, mariner, marry'd to Winifred Burke of the town of Galway, spinster, on the 4th day of November 1796 six, D.Y. Campbell, Vicar

Elias Debutts of Bellfast, marriner, marry'd to Mary Cahil of the town of Galway, spinster, on the 26th day of January 1797 seven, D.Y. Campbell, Vicar

Samuel Robinson of Drumgriffin, miller, marry'd to Eliza Robinson of the town of Galway, spinster, on the 11th day of February 1797 seven, D.Y. Campbell, Vicar

Alexander McDonald, soldier in the Downshire Regiment of Militia, marry'd to Catherine Mellet formerly of Tuam but now of the town of Galway, spinster, on the 20th day of August 1797, D.Y. Campbell, Vicar

[Page] 6

John Herdman, soldier in the Downshire Militia, marry'd to Mary McDonald of the town of Galway, spinster, on the 20th day of August 1797 seven, D.Y. Campbell, Vicar

Michael Donovan of Athunry, dancing master, marry'd to Eliza Griffith of Athunry, spinster, on the 28th day of September 1797 seven, D.Y. Campbell, Vicar

William Davis Junr of Cunnemarra, marry'd to Catherine Keane of Dangan in the county of the town of Galway, spinster, on the 1st day of October 1797 seven, D.Y. Campbell, Vicar

Henry Butler of Millbrook in the County of Clare Esqr, marry'd to Anne Blake, spinster, sister of Walter Blake of Dunmacrine and of Oran Castle Esqr, on the 1st day of January 1798 eight, D.Y. Campbell, Vicar

John Huggard, Quarter Master Serjeant in the Kerry Militia, marry'd to Margaret Mortimer, a widow of the same regiment, on the 7th day of Jany 1798 eight, D.Y. Campbell, Vicar

Walter Blake of Somerville, son of S[i]r Walter Blake Bt, marry'd to Martha Kirwan of Knock alias Hillsbrook in the County of Galway, spinster, on the 5th day of February 1798 eight, D.Y. Campbell, Vicar

William Comyns, armourer to the Perthshire Regt of Fencibles, marry'd to Mary Cox of the town of Galway, spinster, on the 8th day of February 1798 eight, D.Y. Campbell, Vicar

Ronald Cameron, lately a commissioned officer in the Perthshire Regt of Fencibles, marry'd to Eliza Atkison now of Galway, but [former]ly of Forgney in the County of Longford, spinster, on [the] 20th day of April 1798 eight, D.Y. Campbell, Vicar

[Page] 7

Thomas Handcock, soldier in the Perthshire Regt of Highland Fencibles, marry'd to Elizabeth Smyth of Galway, spinster, on the 21st day of April 1798 eight, D.Y. Campbell, Vicar

William Gain, soldier in the Kerry Regt of Militia, marry'd to Sarah Carter of Miltown in the County of Kerry, spinster, on the 13th day of May 1798 eight, D.Y. Campbell, Vicar

William Tyrrell, soldier in the Perthshire Regt of Fencibles, marry'd to Mary Smyth of the town of Galway, spinster, daughter to John Smyth of the same baker, on the 14th day of May 1798 eight, D.Y. Campbell, Vicar

Daniel Thomas, servant to Major General Hutchinson, marry'd to Winnifred Frean of the town of Galway, spinster, on the 20th day of June 1798 eight, D.Y. Campbell, Vicar

Honble Lorenzo Hely Hutchinson Esqr, half pay Major in the Army, brother and aid du camp to Major General Hutchinson, marry'd to Mary Blake of the town of Galway, spinster and eldest daughter of the late Patrick Blake of Drum Esqr, on the 1st day of August 1798 eight, D.Y. Campbell, Vicar

Terence Christie, Private Soldier in the 6th Regt of Foot, marry'd to Elizabeth Hollywood, on the 2nd of August 1798 eight, D.Y. Campbell, Vicar

William Rose Wynter Esqr, Captain in the Suffolk Regt of Fencibles, marry'd to Margaret Purdie, widow of Captn Purdie lately deceased, on the 5th day of November 1798 eight, D.Y. Campbell, Vicar

Reverend Henry Pasley, lately of the city of Dublin, and now curate of Newport in the Diocese of Tuam, marry'd to Lucia Lawton lately of the city of Cork, and now of the county of the town of Galway, spinster, on the 19th day of December 1798 eight, D.Y. Campbell, Vicar

[Page] 8

James Leslie, Serjeant of Grenadiers in the Suffolk Regiment of Fencibles then quartered in Galway, marry'd to Rebecca Caddy, daughter of the late Joseph Caddy, of the town of Galway, spinster, on Monday the 4th day of February 1799 nine, D.Y. Campbell, Vicar

Benjamin Stratford Derinzey, Lieutenant of the Wicklow Regiment of Militia, married to Elizabeth Kelly, daughter of the late Michael Kelly Esqr of Carraroe, spinster, on Tuesday the 4th day of March 1800, John Campbell, Vicar

Jass Laff of the town of Galway, married to Bridget Fitzpatrick, Novr 20th 1799, Jno. Campbell, Vicar

Willm Crawford of the Artillery, married to Anne Eddington, daughter of David Eddington Goaler of the County of Galway, Jany 16th 1800, John Campbell, Vicar

Robt Bakehar, soldier of the Wicklow Militia, married to Catharine Cox, Jany 31st 1800, Jno. Campbell, Vicar

Paul Rubens of the Wicklow Militia, married to Elizabeth Giles, who read her recantation same day, Jany 31st 1800, John Campbell, Vicar

John Donoghue of the town of Galway, married to Sarah Thompson, Decr 29th 1799, Jno. Campbell, Vicar

[Page] 9

Charles Patrick Connolly son of George Connoly, bookseller of the town of Galway, was baptized on the 9th day of March 1800, John Campbell, Vicar

Cornet Willm Clifford of the Carabineers, married to Jane Cormick, niece of S[i]r George Staunton Bart of the Parish of St Nicholas, Galway, May 8th 1800, John Campbell, Vicar

Willm Whitestone, Sergeant of the Waterford Militia, married to Catharine Canavan, daughter of P. Canavan publican in the Parish of St Nicholas, Galway, May 13th 1800, John Campbell, Vicar

Peter Blake Esqr of Corbally, married to Mary Brown, daughter of [blank], on the 30th of April 1800, Robt Shaw, Vicar

Henry Baldwin Esqr, Captn of Artillery, married to Anne Seagrave, daughter of [blank], on the 20th of May 1800, Robt Shaw, Vicar

John Sergeant, Private of the Suffolk Fencibles Regiment of Infantry, married to Sarah Brennan of the town of Galway, on the 7th day of July 1800, John Campbell, Vicar

Benjamin Thomas married to Lucetta Reily of the town of Galway, Sepr 13th 1800, John Campbell, Vicar

Baptised Mary Caddy daughter of Henry Ca[ddy], shoemaker, 28 September 1816, Robt Shaw, Vicar

[Page] 10

Bryan Sweeny, blacksmith, married to Mary Kennedy, on the 29th Septr 1800, John Campbell, Vicar

Joseph Kirwan Esqr of Knock, married to Maria Lynch of Menlogh near Galway, on 24th of Novr 1800, John Campbell, Vicar

David Knight, master of the ship *Riga,* merchant of Dundee, Scotland, married to Alleson Chalmers of Alyith, Scotland, on Wednesday May 6th 1801, John Campbell, Vicar

Martin Richardson of Balinrobe, married to Bridget Lynch of Moycullen, spinster, on Wednesday June 24th 1801, John Campbell, Vicar

Henry Scott of the town of Galway, married to Sarah Evans of the Parish of Balamickward, spinster, on Monday the 7th day of September 1801, John Campbell, Vicar

Dominick Tennant, tidewa[i]ter of the port of Galway, married to Anne Hickey, spinster of the Parish of St Nicholas, Galway, on the 24th day of September 1801, John Campbell, Vicar

John Mahon of the 9th Regiment of Light Dragoons, married to Catharine Hodgens, spinster, daughter of Willm Hodgens, nailor of the town of Galway, John Campbell, Vicar [This entry has no date, presumably the marriage took place between 24 Sept and 29 Oct 1801]

Mathew Donovan, Private of the South Cork Militia, married to Mary Goldtrip of the town of Enniscorthy, spinster, on Thursday October 29th 1801, John Campbell, Vicar

Walter Burke Esqr, Captain of the 62nd Regiment, married to Maria Burke formerly of Gort but now of Galway, spinster, on Monday the 30th day of November 1801, John Campbell, Vicar

[Page] 11

Roderick Macqueen, ensign of the Reay Regiment now quartered in Galway, married to Maria Leech formerly of the city of Dublin but now of the town of Galway, spinster, on Sunday December the sixth 1801, John Campbell, Vicar

Hugh Flanagan of the Parish of Kilcummin, married to Marianne Thomas, daughter of John Thomas Esqr, Sheriff of the town of Galway, spinster, on Saturday Decembr 12th 1801, John Campbell, Vicar

Joseph Morgan, belonging to the South Cork Militia now quartered in Galway, married to Margaret Horan, spinster, daughter of the late Martin Horan of this town shopkeeper, on Friday February the 5th 1802, John Campbell, Vicar

Richard Janns, Revenue Officer of the town of Galway, married to Elizabeth Thomas, daughter of Jno. Thomas Esqr, Sheriff of the town of Galway, on Sunday February the 21st 1802 two, John Campbell, Vicar

William Blair, Lieut of the South Cork Militia quartered here, married to Margaret Walsh, spinster of the town of Galway, on Thursday the 8th day of April 1802 two, John Campbell, Vicar

Charles Bingham, formerly of the 104th Regiment but now of the town of Galway, married to Judith Shields of the town of Galway, spinster, daughter of the late Edmund Shields Esqr, wine merchant, on Thursday April the 22nd 1802 two, John Campbell, Vicar

John Davies of the town of Galway, nailor, married to Rebecca Norman of the town of Galway, spinster, on Wednesday May the nineteenth 1802, John Campbell, Vicar

John Gibson, Drum Major of the Reay Regt of the town of Paisly, Scotland, married to Margaret Cannavan of the town of Galway, spinster, daughter of Peter Cannavan of Market Street Galway, on Saturday July the tenth 1802 two, John Campbell, Vicar

John Mackay of the Reay Regt, married to Mary Kelly of the town of Galway, spinster, on Sunday August the fifteenth 1802, John Campbell, Vicar

William Vinicombe, Private of the 36th Regt of Foot quartered here, married to Jane Mylan of the town of Galway, spinster, on Sunday the 26th of Septr 1802 two, John Campbell, Vicar

[Page] 12

William Concannon Esqr of the Parish of Caltragh, Co Galway, attorney, married to Catharine Browne of the town of Galway, spinster, on Sunday Octr 24th 1802 two, John Campbell, Vicar

Peter Ward Esqr, attorney of the city of Dublin, married to Margaret Morgan of the town of Galway, spinster, on Thursday the 4th day of November 1802 two, John Campbell, Vicar

Daniel Carrick of the Parish of Oranmore, married to Mary Burke of said Parish, spinster, on Monday November the twenty second 1802 two, John Campbell, Vicar

Ebenezer Hills of Savanna in America, Captain of the ship *William Littlejohn,* married to Bridget O'Loughlin of the town of Galway, spinster, on Sunday the fifth day of December 1802 two, John Campbell, Vicar

John Brooks, soldier, married to Mary Macarty, both of the Parish of St Nicholas Galway, on Sunday the 2nd Jany 1803 three, John Campbell, Vicar

Samuel Robinson, taylor, married to Margaret Cox of the town of Galway, spinster, on Thursday Jany 6th 1803, John Campbell, Vicar

Robert Shuffell Esqr of the town of Castlebar, married to Jane Ryan of Galway, a widow, on Saturday Feby 5th 1803, John Campbell, Vicar

Thomas Farrington of Galway, married to Elizabeth Cunningham, spinster, on Tuesday February 22nd 1803 also on the same day Digby Devenish Esqr of Galway, married to Elizabeth Digby of Arran, spinster, John Campbell, Vicar

Richard Jackson, Private of the 36th Regt, married to Susan O'Brian of Galway, spinster, on Thursday March 19th 1803 three, John Campbell, Vicar

William Davis, Private of the 36th Regt, married to Nancy Machanally, spinster, on Tuesday April 12th 1803 three, John Campbell, Vicar

Richard Knowles, Private of the 36th Regt, married to Diana Bankes of Galway, spinster, on Tuesday April the 12th 1803, John Campbell, Vicar

Henry Short, soldier of the 36th Regt of Foot, married to Charlotte Goggin of Galway, spinster, on Sunday May 15th 1803, John Campbell, Vicar

[Page] 13

William Wardsworth, Corporal & acting Sergeant of the 36 Regiment of Foot, married to Bridget Campbell, daughter of James Campbell of Galway, Revenue Officer, on Sunday the nineteenth day of June 1803 three, John Campbell, Vicar

Robert Buchannan Esqr of Westport, Captn of the revenue cruizer, married to Jane Neligan of the town of Galway, spinster, on Wednesday June the 22nd 1803 three, John Campbell, Vicar

Thomas Griffiths, acting Sergeant of the 36th Regt of Foot, married to Heelen Magan of the town of Galway, spinster, on Wednesday June the 29th 1803 three, John Campbell, Vicar

Benjamin Grandy, Sergeant of the 36th Regt of Foot, married to Jane McNabb of Galway, spinster, on Thursday Decr 11th 1803, John Campbell, Vicar

Thomas Kine Esqr of Cregg County of Galway but now of the town of Galway, married to Anne Devenish alias Warren, of Galway, widow, on Thursday January 12th 1804 four, John Campbell, Vicar

Thomas Turner Esqr of the 17th Light Dragoons, married to Barbara Eleanor Blake of Menlogh, spinster, on Sunday the 25th of March 1804 four, John Campbell, Vicar

Barttelott Smyth, Lieut of the 25th Regt of Foot, married to Elizabeth Skerrett of Galway, spinster, on Wednesday the 28th March 1804 four, John Campbell, Vicar

George Stirling of the town of Galway, Revenue Officer, married to Mary Burk of Galway, spinster, on Saturday the fourteenth of July 1804 four, John Campbell, Vicar

William Jeffers of Galway, shoemaker, married to Catherine Timms of Galway, widow, on Sunday August 5th 1804 four, John Campbell, Vicar

John Taggart, shoemaker, of Galway married to Mary Stewart of Galway, spinster, on Monday Novr 5th 1804 four, John Campbell, Vicar

Sunday March 3rd 1805 five, Richard Mortimer of Galway, baker, married to Catherine Lee, daughter of Stephen Lee of said town mercht, Jno. Campbell, Vicar

Thomas Trumble, Lieut of the Sligo Militia, married to Bridget Skerrett of Aran but now of Galway, on Wednesday July the 10th 1805 five, John Campbell, Vicar

George Wheeler of the town of Galway, ropemaker, married to Ellen Dillon, daughter of Thos Dillon, glover, on Monday 18th Novr 1805, John Campbell, Vicar

John Cox Junr of the town of Galway, shoemaker, married to Eleanor Slammion of Galway, spinster, on Tuesday Decr 24th 1805 five, John Campbell, Vicar

[Page] 14

William Rutherford, Private of Captain Walker's Light Company 26th Regt of Foot, married to Bridget Byrne of Galway, spinster, on Monday the 27th of January 1806 six, John Campbell, Vicar

William Gray, Lieut of the 30th Regt of Foot, married to Barbara Elizabeth Blake, daughter of Thos Blake of Blake Hill, Co Galway, on Monday Jany 27th 1806 six, John Campbell, Vicar

Thomas Cox of the town of Galway, married to Sabina Martin of Galway, on Monday the 10th day of February 1806 six, John Campbell, Vicar

Sunday April 27th 1806 six, William Mason of the town of Galway, married to Elizabeth Adam, daughter of Robert Adams of Galway merchant, John Campbell, Vicar

Saturday May 31st 1806 six, Rickard O'Connell, Assistant Surgeon of the Light Batallion quartered in Galway, married to Elizabeth Bryce, spinster, sister of Lady Blake of Menlo near Galway, John Campbell, Vicar

Wednesday June 4th 1806 six, William Vere Taylor, Lieut of the 28th Regt of Foot 1st Batallion, married to Clare Bellew, daughter of John Bellew of Galway Esqr, John Campbell, Vicar

Thursday July the 3rd 1806 six, Thomas Lackey of Galway, ropemaker, married to Bridget O'Donnell of Galway, spinster, John Campbell, Vicar

Saturday July the 5th 1806 six, Thomas Lyster of Galway Esqr, married to Harriot Burk of Galway, spinster, John Campbell, Vicar

Saturday Septr 13th 1806 six, Dominick Burke of Galway married to Cherry Groom of Charleville, spinster, John Campbell, Vicar

Saturday Septr 27th, William Wheeler of Galway, ropemaker, married to Mary Jones of sd place, spinster, John Campbell, Vicar

Sunday Septr 28th 1806 six, James Kelly, Private of Artillery drivers, married to Eleanor Carson of Galway, spinster, John Campbell, Vicar

Sunday February 8th 1807 seven, George Cottingham of Galway, brushmaker, married to Mary Murphy of Galway, spinster, John Campbell, Vicar

Saturday July 4th 1807 seven, Luke Dodgworth of Galway, Revenue Offic[er], married to Mary Lynch of sd town, spinster, John Campbell, Vicar

[Page] 15

[For baptisms May 1800 - Jan 1808 see loose pages and pages (1) – (12) at the end of the register]

Sunday February 7th 1808, baptized Martha daughter of Wm Blair, Lieutenant of the South Cork Regt of Militia, John Campbell, Vicar
Sunday Feby 14th 1808, baptized John son of William McCullogh of the town of Galway, nailor, John Campbell, Vicar
Sunday February 28th 1808 eight, John Pugh of the town of Galway married to Mary Field of sd town spinster, John Campbell, Vicar
Thursday March 3rd 1808, baptized Robert son of Henry Scott of the town of Galway, cabinet maker, John Campbell, Vicar
Revd Thomas Wade, master of Erasmus Smith Schools, was married to Sarah Hamilton of Galway, widow, by the Revd L.Younge, Vicar of Kilcolgan, by permission of the Vicar of Galway, on Sunday the twentieth day of March 1808 eight, John Campbell, Vicar
Monday April 18th 1808, baptized John son of John Shaw of the west suburbs of Galway, tanner, John Campbell, Vicar
Sunday May 1st 1808, Charles Peshill, Captain of 88th Regt of Foot, married to Letitia Martin of Clareville, spinster, daughter of Richard Martin M.P. Esqr of Balinahinch, John Campbell, Vicar
Friday May 20th 1808, baptized Thomas Edward son of Richard O'Connell, Assistant Surgeon in the Army, John Campbell, Vicar
Saturday May 28th 1808 eight, baptized William son of John Bebbs, Sergeant of his M[ajesty's] 6th Regiment of Foot, John Campbell, Vicar
Sunday June 26th 1808, baptized Joseph son of Henry Bright of the west suburbs Galway, John Campbell, Vicar
Tuesday June 28th 1808, baptized Henry son of Willm Mason Esqr, one of the Sheriffs of Galway, John Campbell, Vicar
Tuesday August 2nd 1808, baptized Mary daughter of John Monaghan of Galway, porter, John Campbell, Vicar
Tuesday August 16th 1808 eight, baptized Hannah daughter of John Gibbons of Galway, merchant, John Campbell, Vicar
Sunday August 21st 1808, baptized James son of Duncan Cameron of Eyrefield Esqr, John Campbell, Vicar

Monday Septr 5th 1808, baptized David John son of Dominick Tennant of Galway, Revenue Officer, John Campbell, Vicar
Tuesday Septr 7th 1808, baptized Anne daughter of James Francis of the West, papermaker, John Campbell, Vicar
[Sunday] 25th [no month] 1808, Robert son of Captain Robt O'Brien of Prospect was baptized by the Rev L.H.Younge by permission, John Campbell, Vicar
By permission of the Revd John Campbell, Vicar of Galway, on Tuesday 18th of October 1808, Anna Maria Rose daughter of Wm Rose Winter of the town of Galway was baptized by the Revd J.Wade, John Campbell Vi[car], the child was 18 months old
Sunday Novr 5th 1808, baptized Mary daughter of Thomas Farrington of the West, G[alway?], John Campbell, Vicar

[Page] 16

Saturday Novr 12th 1808, baptized Catharine daughter of John Conolly of the west suburbs Galway, John Campbell, Vicar
Sunday Novr 27th 1808, baptized Elleanor daughter of George Wheeler of the town of Galway, ropemaker, John Campbell, Vicar
Same day baptized Agnes daughter of John Egan, of the 7th Garrison Bata[lion], same day baptized Esther daughter of Henry Smith of Galway, brazier, John Campbell, Vicar
Sunday Decr 11th 1808, Anne daughter of John Griffith baptized, John Campbell, Vicar
Sunday Jany 8th 1809, Joseph Mortimer, Chief Mate of the *Townsend* revenue cruizer, married to Bridget Eddington of the town of Galway, spinster, by John Campbell, Vicar
Sunday Jany 15th 1809, baptized George son of John Lackey of the town of Galway, ropemaker, John Campbell, Vicar
Tuesday Jany 31st 1809, baptized Elizabeth Margaret daughter of Digby Devenish, Revenue Officer, John Campbell, Vicar
Thursday February 2nd 1809, baptized Marcella daughter of Richard Pear of Galway, John Campbell, Vicar
Thursday Feby 23rd 1809, baptized Maria Agnes daughter of Richard Creuston of Galway, mariner, John Campbell, Vicar
Thursday March 9th 1809, baptized Marianne daughter of Henry Scott

of Galway, cabinet maker, John Campbell, Vicar

Tuesday March 14th 1809, baptized Stephen son of Michael McDonogh of Galway, shopkeeper, John Campbell, Vicar

Friday April 28 1809, Terence O'Neill, Captain of sev[eral] fencibles, married to Heelena French of the town of Galway, widow, John Campbell, Vicar

Sunday May 28th 1809, baptized Thomas Lyster son of Henry Parker, Captain of the 53rd Regt of Foot, John Campbell, Vicar

Thursday June 7th 1809, baptized Edward Bryce son of Sir John Blake of Menlo Bart, John Campbell, Vicar

Sunday July 9th 1809, baptized Mary daughter of Lieut Deal of the R[oyal] Navy, same day baptized Anne daughter of John Cox of Galway, shoemaker, John Campbell, Vicar

Sunday July 16th 1809, baptized Elizabeth daughter of Michl Smyth, formerly Sergt of the Galway Militia, John Campbell, Vicar

Tuesday August 15th 1809, baptized William son of Andrew Robinson of Galway, jeweller, John Campbell, Vicar

Sunday Octr 8th 1809, baptized Willm Joseph son of William Mason, one of the sheriffs of the town of Galway, John Campbell, Vicar

Wednesday Novr 1st 1809, baptized John son of John Taggart of Galway, shoemaker, John Campbell, Vicar

[Page] 17

Friday Novr 10th 1809, baptized Elizabeth daughter of John Shawe of the west suburbs Galway, John Campbell, Vicar

Sunday Novr 16th 1809, baptized Jesse son of Jesse Shawe of the town of Galway, cabinet maker, John Campbell, Vicar

Sunday December 17th 1809 nine, baptized Willm son of Henry Latty of Galway, musick master, John Campbell, Vicar

Monday Jany 22nd 1810 ten, baptized Michael son of Patrick Hearn of Galway, shoemaker, John Campbell, Vicar

Thursday March 1st 1810, baptized Jane daughter of Duncan Cameron of Eyreville near Galway, John Campbell, Vicar

Sunday March 18th 1810, baptized Francis son of Henry Persse of Newcastle near Galway, John Campbell, Vicar

Sunday April 1st 1810, baptized Frances daughter of Henry Scott of Galway, cabinet maker, John Campbell, Vicar

Thursday May 3rd 1810, baptized Marianne daughter of Joseph Mortimer, Chief Mate of the *Townsend* revenue cruizer, John Campbell, Vicar

Sunday May 6th, baptized Frances Lucinda daughter of Thomas Evans of Galway, also same day were married by me, Thomas Hubbart & Marianne Scott, spinster, both of the town of Galway, John Campbell, Vicar

Sunday June 17th 1810, baptized Jane daughter of John Corbett, Surveyor of Excise of Galway, John Campbell, Vicar

Sunday July 29th 1810, baptized Rodolphus Richard Thomas son of Captn James Marshal of west suburbs, John Campbell, Vicar

Sunday August 19th 1810, baptized Catharine daughter of John Griffith of Galway, shoemaker, John Campbell, Vicar

Wednesday September 5th 1810, baptized Anne daughter of George McArthy, [musician][36] of the town of Galway, John Campbell, Vicar

Wednesday Septr 12th 1810, baptized John son of John Storey, sailmaker, John Campbell, Vicar

Thursday October 11th 1810, baptized Susana Maria daughter of Benjamin Thomas of Galway, John Campbell, Vicar

Friday October 12th 1810, baptized Elizabeth daughter of Joseph Lewis, John Campbell, Vicar

Sunday Novr 25th 1810, baptized Anne daughter of Mich Smyth, Sergeant of the 51st Regiment of Foot, John Campbell, Vicar

Sunday Decr 16th 1810, baptized Eliza daughter of John Lackey, ropemaker of the West & same day Bridget daughter of Henry Bright of the west road, nailor, John Campbell, Vicar

[Page] 18

Monday Decr 24th, baptized Andrew Pitman son of Andrew Robinson of Galway, jeweller, John Campbell, Vicar

Thursday Decr 27 1810, baptized Joseph son of John Loney, Private of the Tipperary Regt of Militia also same day baptized Thomas son of Digby Devenish of Aran, John Campbell, Vicar

Tuesday Jany 8th 1811, baptized George son of Wm Mason, one of the sheriffs of the town of Galway, John Campbell, Vicar

---

[36] See page 20 of the register where there is a reference to George Macarthy, Professor of Music, in an entry dated 29 May 1814.

Wednesday Feby 13[th] 1811, baptized Mary daughter of Vescy McCarrol, tidewa[i]ter of Galway, John Campbell, Vicar

Sunday Feby 17[th] 1811, baptized Elizabeth daughter of George Wheeler of the east suburbs, John Campbell, Vicar

Sunday Feby 24[th] 1811, baptized Mary daughter of J. Harris, of Tipperary Rgt which infant Tuesday 6[th] March burd [buried], John Campbell, Vicar

Sunday March 3rd 1811, baptized John son of Thos Hubbett of Galway, shoemaker, John Campbell, Vicar

Sunday March 17th 1811, baptized Anne daughter of John Shaw of the West, carrier, John Campbell, Vicar

Friday April 5th 1811, baptized Anne daughter of John Whiteheir, of the 56th Regt now recruiting in Galway, John Campbell, Vicar

Sunday April 7[th] 1811, baptized John [son] of Sam Robinson, taylor of Galway, John Campbell, Vicar

Sunday 21[st] April 1811, baptized Henry Robt son of Reuben Hughes Esqr of Dominick St, John Campbell, Vicar

Tuesday June 25[th] 1811, baptized John son of Sir Jno. Blake of Menlo Ba[r]t, John Campbell, Vicar

Sunday June 30[th] 1811, baptized John son of Wm Given, Tyrone Militia, John Campbell, Vicar

Thursday July 4[th] 1811, baptized Lucinda daughter of Thos Burke of Galway, po[st]master, John Campbell, Vicar

Sunday July 14[th] 1811, baptized Mary daughter of Wm Phillips, Sergeant of the Tyrone Militia, John Campbell, Vicar

Wednesday July 17[th] 1811, baptized Richard son of Thos Farrington of the west suburbs Galway, John Campbell, Vicar

Saturday August 17[th] 1811, baptized James son of Herbert Lennen, Private of the Tyrone Militia, John Campbell, Vicar

Wedneday October 23rd 1811, baptized Mary daughter of Patt Heavy of the east suburbs Galway, coachmaker, John Campbell, Vicar

Sunday Novr 3 1811, baptized Agnes daughter of James Richardson, Private of the Tyrone Regt of Militia & also baptized Elizabeth daughter of Wm Leeson, Sergeant of sd regiment, John Campbell, Vicar

Saturday Novr 10th 1811, baptized Ellen Agnes daughter of William Wheeler of the east suburbs, ropemaker, John Campbell, Vicar

Saturday Novr 16th 1811, baptized Anne daughter of James Frances of the west suburbs, paper maker, John Campbell, Vicar

Tuesday [no date] February 1812, baptized Anne daughter of Wilkins Simcockes Esqr, John Campbell, Vicar

[Page] 19

[For other baptismal entries for 1812 see page (6) at the end of the register]

Sunday February 23rd 1812, baptized Sarah daughter of Jesse Shaw of Galway, cabinet maker, John Campbell, Vicar

Galway November 28th 1809, John Storey, sailmaker an[d] Elizabeth Graves, spinster, both of the town of Galway, were joined together in holy matrimony, by the Revd Robert Shaw, one of the Vicars of Galway, John Campbell, Vicar

Sunday April 5th 1812, baptized Henry son of John Taggart, shoemaker, John Campbell, Vicar

Sunday April 26th 1812, baptized Maria daughter of John Griffith, shoemaker, John Campbell, Vicar

Thursday Novr 19th 1812, baptized Robert Brice son of Sir John Blake of Menlo Bart, John Campbell, Vicar

Tuesday Decr 8th 1812, baptized Mathew son of John O'Brien of the Mail Coach Office, Galway, John Campbell, Vicar

Tuesday Jany 26th 1813, baptized William son of Thomas Mathews, Private of the Westmoreland Regt of Militia, John Campbell, Vicar

Friday Jany 29th 1813, baptized John son of Marcy McCarrol of the town of Galway, Revenue Officer, John Campbell, Vicar

Tuesday Feby 2nd 1813, Henry Caddy of Galway, shoemaker and Mary Bulger of the same, spinster, were joined together in holy matrimony, in the Parish Church of St Nicholas, Galway, by me, John Campbell, Vicar

Sunday April 4th 1813, baptized Bridget daughter of Henry Bright of the west suburbs Galway, John Campbell, Vicar

Thursday April 15th 1813, baptized Sarah daughter of Jesse Shawe, cabinet maker, John Campbell, Vicar

Monday May 10th 1813, baptized Jane daughter of John McCully of the west suburbs Galway, John Campbell, Vicar

Sunday May 30th 1813, baptized Letitia Maria daughter of Ulick O'Bri[en] near Galway, John Campbell, Vicar
Friday July 16th 1813, baptized George - Robert son of Thomas Conolly of the town of Galway, bookbinder, John Campbell, Vicar
Sunday July 18th 1813, baptized John son of George Wheeler of the town of Galway, ropemaker, John Campbell, Vicar
Saturday July 24th 1813, baptized Anne daughter of Digby Devenish of Aron, John Campbell, Vicar
Wednesday Septr 8th 1813, baptized Charlotte daughter of Henry Scott of Galway, cabinet maker, John Campbell, Vicar
Saturday Septr 11 1813, John Bradley of Galway, Revenue Officer and Cathe[rine] Bath of sd town, spinster, were joined together in holy matrimony, by me, John Campbell, Vicar
Sunday Octr 31st 1813, baptized Mary daughter of Henry Harms of the Mainguard, Galway, shopkeeper, John Campbell, Vicar

[Page] 20

Sunday morning Novr 5th 1813, baptized Elizabeth daughter of Richd Peare of Bridge St, Galway, merchant, John Campbell, Vicar
Monday Novr 8th 1813, Hubert Manning of Galway, dancing master and Anne Murphy of sd town, spinster, were joined together in holy matrimony, in the Parish Church of St Nicholas this morning, by me, John Campbell, Vicar of Galway
Monday Novr 29th 1813, baptized Elizabeth daughter of Willm Mason of the town of Galway, Revenue Officer, John Campbell, Vicar
Sunday Decr 26th 1813, baptized Benjamin Bloomfield son of Benjamin Thomas of the Excise Office, Galway, John Campbell, Vicar
Wednesday Feby 3rd 1814, baptized Emelia daughter of Thomas Hubbert of Galway, shoemaker, John Campbell, Chaplain
Sunday February 6th 1814, baptized Samuel Wilkins son of Wilkins Simcockes of Galway Esqr, same day baptized Heelen daughter of James Heavy of Moate, coachmaker, John Campbell, Vicar
Sunday Febr 29th 1814, baptized Righteous Faithfull son of Wiggen, soldier Berkshire Militia, also same day baptized Richard son of John Griffith of Galway, shoemaker, John Campbell, Vicar

Thursday March 3rd, baptized John son of John O'Brien, agent of the Mail Coach Office, Meyrick Square[37], John Campbell, Vicar

Monday April 4th 1814, baptized Mary Anne daughter of John Kenny of Custom Gap, Galway, nailer, John Campbell, Vicar

Sunday April 10th 1814, baptized Launcey daughter of George Preston [?] of Galway, smith, John Campbell, Vicar

Friday April 15th 1814, baptized Joseph son of Henry Caddy of Galway, shoemaker, John Campbell, Vicar

Sunday May 15th 1814, baptized Ellen daughter of Thos Farrington, attendant at present at the Salmon Weir, John Campbell, Vicar

Sunday May 29th 1814, baptized Thomas son of Thomas Gaskins, Private Berkshire Militia, same day Harriot daughter of George Macarthy of Galway, Professor of Musick, same day Thomas son of John Taggart of Galway, shoemaker, John Campbell, Vicar

Friday June 24th 1814, baptized Thomas son of Reuben Hughe of Dominick St, paper maker, John Campbell, Vicar

[Page] 21

Monday July 4th 1814, William Birchen, Private in the Royal Berkshire Regiment of Militia and Sabina Holleran of the Parish of Saint Nicholas, Galway, spinster, were joined together in holy matrimony in sd Church, by me, John Campbell, Vicar

Sunday July 10th 1814, baptized Thomas son of Thomas James, Sergeant of the King's County Militia, John Campbell, Vicar

Sunday July 17th 1814, Samuel Simcockes of the town of Galway, mercht and Elizabeth Francis Hutchinson of sd town, spinster, daughter of John Francis Hutchinson of the Salmon Weir, were joined together in holy matrimony, in the Parish Church of St Nicholas, by me, John Campbell, Vicar

Same day baptized Charles son of Varsy McCarrol of the town of Galway, Revenue Officer, John Campbell, Vicar

Thursday July 21st 1814, John Austin, Lieutenant of the Royal Berkshire Militia quartered at Galway and Bridgelina O'Shaughnessy of Galway, were joined together in holy matrimony, in the Parish Church of St Nicholas, Galway, by me, John Campbell, Vicar

---

[37] The Green in the centre of Galway was known as Meyrick Square from 1801 until 1820, when it was renamed Eyre Square, see Paul Walsh, *Discover Galway* (Dublin, 2001).

Wednesday August 3rd 1814, baptized Patrick son of Patrick Holly of Bohermore, mason, John Campbell, Vicar

Sunday August 7th 1814, baptized John Frances son of Nicholas Lynch of the church yard, John Campbell, Vicar

Tuesday Septr 6th, baptized Eliza daughter of Vescy Daniel of Church Lane, dyer, John Campbell, Vicar

Sunday September 25th 1814, baptized Henry son of Heubert Manning of Galway, dancing master, John Campbell, Vicar

Sunday October 2nd 1814, baptized Michael son of James Galagher, soldier of the 88th Regt Foot also baptized Mary and Margaret two foundlings, John Campbell, Vicar

Thursday October 20th 1814, Hugh McPherson, Sergeant of the 74th Regiment of Foot and Mary Caddy of the town of Galway, spinster, were joined together in holy matrimony, in the Church of St Nicholas, Galway, by John Campbell, Vicar

[Page] 22

Gave private baptism to Walter Blake Lawrence at Merlin Park, on Monday the 21st of November 1814, he being declared ill, James Daly [first entry by Rev James Daly, Warden of Galway 1811-1864]

Sunday Decr 25 1814, baptized John Charles Annesly son of Richard Annesly Joynt of the Roscommon Militia Esqr, John Campbell, Vicar

Tuesday Decr 27th 1814, baptized Jane daughter of Henry Scott of Galway, cabinet maker, John Campbell, Vicar

Sunday January 1st 1815, baptized John son of Michael McDonogh of Galway, school master, John Campbell, Vicar

Thursday January 12th 1815, baptized Digby son of Digby Devenish of Aron Esqr, John Campbell, Vicar

Sunday Jany 15th 1815, baptized Jane daughter of John Storey of Galway, sailmaker, John Campbell, Vicar

Sunday Jany 22nd 1815, baptized Margaret daughter of Duncan Cameron Esqr of Bath Lodge near Galway, John Campbell, Vicar

Sunday February the 5th 1815, David Smith of Galway, nailor and Mary Joy of sd Parish, widow, were joined together in holy matrimony, by me, John Campbell, Vicar

Tuesday February 21st 1815, baptized John son of William Prosser, Private of the Tipperary Regt of Militia, John Campbell, Vicar

Sunday March 5th, baptized John son of Jno. Lackey of the town of Galway, ropemaker, John Campbell, Vicar, same day baptized George son of George Cuppadge Esqr of the Custom House, Galway, John Campbell, Vicar

Thursday March 23rd 1815, baptized Christian Ralph son of Henry Harms of Galway, grocer, John Campbell, Vicar

Sunday April 16th 1815, baptized Maria daughter of Richard Peare of Westbridge Galway, John Campbell, Vicar

[Page] 23

Wednesday May 17th 1815, baptized Thomas son of George Washinton Cole, Revenue Officer of the port of Galway, John Campbell, Vicar

Sunday July 9th 1815, baptized the following children viz Cecilia a foundling, Letitia daughter of John O'Brien of the Mail Coach Office, George Eyre son of Samuel Simcockes Esqr, John Campbell, Vicar

Sunday July 23rd 1815, baptized Jane daughter of John Griffith, shoemaker, John Campbell, Vicar

Sunday August 6th 1815, baptized the following children viz Mary a foundling, Diana daughter of Henry Bright of the west suburbs, nailor and John son of Robert Goodfellow, Corporal of the 74th Regt of Foot, John Campbell, Vicar

Wednesday August 16th 1815, baptized Thomas son of Jesse Shaw of Galway, cabinet maker, John Campbell, Vicar

Wednesday Septr 6th 1815, baptized Bloomfield son of Benjamin Thomas of the Excise Office, Galway, John Campbell, Vicar

Sunday February 4th 1816, baptized John son of John Kenny of the east suburbs Galway, nailor, John Campbell, Vicar

Wednesday February 6th 1816, gave private baptism to John Henry Blake, born January 20th 1816, son of Henry Martin Blake of Windfield Esqr, John Campbell, Vicar

Sunday February 11th 1816, baptized Mathias a foundling, also on the same day baptized James son of David Hamilton of the Waterford Militia, John Campbell, Vicar

Monday March 25th Do, baptized Elizabeth Mary daughter of James Simpson, belonging to the stonemasons of the lighthouse now building at Mutton Island, John Campbell, Vicar

45

Wednesday April 3rd 1816, baptized Edward son of Reuben Hughes of Dominick St, Galway, paper maker, John Campbell, Vicar

Sunday April 14th 1816, baptized Redmond Mortimer son of Charles Eddington of Galway, John Campbell, Vicar

Thursday May 16th 1816, baptized Davis son of John McColough of the east suburbs of Galway, nailor, John Campbell, Vicar

Friday May 24th 1816, baptized Elizabeth daughter of Wilkins Simcockes of Galway Esqr, John Campbell, Vicar

Sunday May 26th 1816, baptized Joseph son of Ralph Walsh of Galway, stocking weaver, John Campbell, Vicar

Friday May 31st 1816, baptized Eliza daughter of William Wheeler of Bohermore, Galway, rope maker, John Campbell, Vicar

Sunday June 16th 1816, baptized Anne daughter of Jno. Taggart of Galway, shoemaker, John Campbell, Vicar

Thursday June 27th 1816, baptized Charles son of Wm McConne[ll?] of Galway, coachmaker, John Campbell, Vicar

Sunday June 30th 1816, baptized William son of Thos Hubb[ert] of Galway, shoemaker, John Campbell, Vicar

[Page] 24

Sunday July 21st 1816, baptized Harriot daughter of Nicholas Lynch of Galway, John Campbell, Vicar

Thursday July 25th 1816, baptized James son of John Fitzimons, Governor of the County Goal of Galway, John Campbell, Vicar

Sunday August 18th 1816, baptized Thomas son of Thomas Farrington, belonging to the Salmon Weir, John Campbell, Vicar

Sunday Septr 1st 1816, baptized Sabina daughter of Samuel Simcockes of Galway, merchant, John Campbell, Vicar

Monday Septr 2nd 1816, baptized Eliza daughter of John Griffiths of Carm[or]e near Galway, John Campbell, Vicar

Sunday Novr 3rd 1816, baptized Celia daughter of Wm Mason of Galway, coast officer, John Campbell, Vicar

Sunday Novr 24th 1816, baptized Margaret daughter of John Robinson, instrument maker, John Campbell, Vicar

Sunday Decr 8th 1816, baptized William son of George Cuppaidge, pro Collector of Galway, John Campbell, Vicar

Friday February 7th 1817, baptized Rose daughter of Patrick Kennedy, guard of the mail coach, John Campbell, Vicar

Wednesday February 19th 1817, baptized Margaret daughter of Michael McDonogh, schoolmaster, John Campbell, Vicar

Sunday March 9th, baptized William son of William Forbes of Bohermore, Galway, John Campbell, Vicar

Sunday March 16th 1817, baptized Mathew son of Edward Millmay of Bohermore, Galway, John Campbell, Vicar

Thursday May 15th 1817, baptized Henry Daniel son of Henry Suffield of the College, Galway, John Campbell, Vicar [Erasmus Smith School, known as the 'College']

Saturday May 31st Do, baptized William son of John Storey of Galway, sailmaker, John Campbell, Vicar

Sunday August 31st 1817, baptized Jane daughter of James Moffet, master gunner, John Campbell, Vicar

Monday Septr 15th Do, baptized Henrietta Frances daughter of Digby Devenish of Aron, Revenue Officer, John Campbell, Vicar

Tuesday Septr 16th 1817, William Reed, soldier 2nd Batallion of 12th Regt of Foot and Elizabeth Tighe, spinster, were joined together in holy matrimony, in the Church of St Nicholas, Galway, by me, John Campbell, Vicar

[Page] 25

Wednesday Septr 17th 1817, baptized William son of W Chislett, Private of 2nd Battalion 12th Regt of Foot, John Campbell, Vicar

Saturday Septr 20th 1817, baptized John son of George Washington Cole, Revenue Officer of the port of Galway, John Campbell, Vicar

Sunday Septr 1817, baptized Francis Joseph son of Nicholas Lynch of Galway, cloth merchant, John Campbell, Vicar

Wednesday Septr 24th 1817, William Wilson, soldier of the 12th Regt of Foot, Margaret Conneely of Galway, spinster, were joined together in holy matrimony, by me, John Campbell, Vicar

Sunday Septr 28th 1817, baptized Mary Jane daughter of George Washinton Bursteed of Cottage, Dangan, Galway, John Campbell, Vicar

Monday Septr 29th 1817, David Ramage, soldier of the 12th Regt of Foot and Honor Lenaghan, widow, were joined together in holy matrimony, by me, John Campbell, Vicar

Monday October 13th 1817, Henry Stephens of Blennerville, Co of Kerry Esqr and Eliza Hacker of Galway, widow, were joined together in holy matrimony, by me, John Campbell, Vicar

Wednesday October 15th 1817, Peter Dyer, soldier of the 12th Regt of Foot and Sarah Shaughnessy of Galway, spinster, were joined together in holy matrimony, by me, John Campbell, Vicar

Sunday October the 19th 1817, baptized a Parish child by name Luke, also baptized James son of Henry Bright of the west suburbs, nailor, also baptized Harriet daughter of John O'Brien of the Mail Coach Office Bohermore, John Campbell, Vicar

Monday October 21st 1817, Patrick Mullen of Ballimac Gibbon, Co Mayo and Bridget Leonard of Kentville near Galway, were joined together in holy matrimony, by me, in the Collegiate Church of St Nicholas, Galway, John Campbell, Vicar

Sunday Novr 2nd 1817, baptized Mary daughter of John Watts, Private 12th Regt of Foot, John Campbell, Vicar

Saturday Novr 8th 1817, Joseph Borradaele, Sergeant of 12th Regt of Foot and Agnes Lynch of Galway, were joined together in holy matrimony, by me, in the Collegiate Church of St Nicholas, Galway, John Campbell, Vicar

Sunday Novr 9th 1817, baptized Henry son of William Stephens, Private 12th Regt of Foot, John Campbell, Vicar

Same day baptized Mary Anne daughter of Alexander Browne, Sergeant of 12th Regiment of Foot, John Campbell, Vicar

[Page] 26

John Wheeler & Margaret French, both of the Parish, were married after banns duly published, October 6th 1817, by me, James Daly, Warden

Sunday Novr 9th 1817, baptized Mary daughter of Duncan Cameron Esqr, Tide Surveyor of Galway, John Campbell, Vicar

Thursday Novr 13th 1817, Joseph Gunton of Leicester, stocking weaver and Catharine Carthy of Loughrea spinster, were joined together in holy matrimony, by me, in the Collegiate Church of St Nicholas, John Campbell, Vicar

Monday Novr 17th 1817, baptized James son Wm Wakefield, Private 12th Regt of Foot, John Campbell, Vicar

Sunday Novr 23rd 1817, baptized Elizabeth daughter of George Fry, Private 12th Regt of Foot, John Campbell, Vicar

Wednesday Novr 26th 1817, baptized William son of William Waters, pensioner, John Campbell, Vicar

Saturday Novr 29th 1817, John Tiernan of Galway, hatter and Bridget Hart of sd Parish, were joined together in holy matrimony, by me, in the Collegiate Church of St Nicholas, John Campbell, Vicar

Thursday Decr 4th 1817, baptized John son of William Sherwood, Sergeant Major of 12th Regt of Foot, John Campbell, Vicar

Wednesday Decr 17th 1817, baptized Mary daughter of Edward Sewell, Private of 12th Regt of Foot, John Campbell, Vicar

Tuesday Decr 23rd 1817, baptized Charlotte daughter of Captain John Cripp Dennis of Galway, John Campbell, Vicar

Thursday Decr 25th 1817, Joseph Hugh Montgomery of Belleville, Co of Galway Esqr and Ruth Goodman of Galway, widow, were joined together in holy matrimony, in the Collegiate Church of St Nicholas, by me, John Campbell, Vicar

Sunday Decr 28th 1817, baptized John son of Richard Peare of Bridge St, Galway, John Campbell, Vicar

Sunday Jany 4th 1818, baptized Edward son of Benjamin Brearly, Corporal of the 84th Regt of Foot, John Campbell, Vicar

Sunday Jany 11th 1818, Hugh Duncan, mate of the sloop *Active* of Liverpool and Ellen Mortimer of Galway, spinster, were married by me, in St Nicholas Church, John Campbell, Vicar [below this entry, alongside the signature of John Campbell, in a different ink is the following entry]:

dying write I this.

[Page] 27

Baptized Mary Parker, Febry 25th 1818, Jas Daly
Baptized William Shaw, March 4th 1818, Jas Daly
Rawdon Macnamara & Mary Symmers were married in this Church, by license, March 11th 1818, by me, James Daly
Witness: Geo Symmers   Jno. Steadman, Clarke

Baptized Jas Dunleavy, April 1st 1818, Jas Daly
Baptized James Edmund Cubbage, October 8th 1818, Jas Daly
Miss Anne Smyth buried by me, Octr 18th 1818, James Daly
Patrick & Catharine Newel were married by me, November 9th 1818, James Daly
Witness Jno. Steadman
Baptized Maria Scott, November 11th 1818
Baptized Arthur Edington, Decr 20th 1818, James Daly
Baptized Miss Christian Shone, January 27th 1819, James Daly
Edward Righton & Jane Fitzpatrick were married after banns duly published, by me, on the 15th of February 1819, James Daly   Witness James Cullen

[Page] 28

April 2 1819, baptized Margaret Kennedy, Jas Daly
April 14 1819, James McCulla & Mary Cole were married, in the Collegiate Chapel of Galway, after banns duly published, by me, James Daly   Witness Andr Rud, John McCulla
April 15 1819, Robert Jackson and Winifred Kilroy married in the Collegiate Chapel of Galway (by license), by me, Edwd Burke, Vicar Witness Jno. Steadman, Jno. O'Brien
Robert Fitzgerald and Elenor O Flaherty married by me, on the twenty fifth day of December one thousand eight hundred & eighteen, Edwd Burke, Vicar   Witness Jno. Steadman
Registered 15th April 1819, E[dward] B[urke]
7th May Charles O Donnell[38] and Mary Nolan married in the Collegiate Chapel of St Nicholas, Galway, by license, by me, Edwd Burke, Vicar
Jno. Steadman [Witness]

[Page] 29

Hugh Roberts & Honora Ram married after banns duly published, by me, February 6th 1818, James Daly
Gave private baptism to Anastasia Lawrence, September 181[9], Jas Daly
Baptized Elizabeth Boyd, November 8th 1818, James Daly

---

[38] Originally written McDonnell.

James Martin & Mary Smyth were married by me, after banns duly published, 26th of January 1819, James Daly

Baptized J. Daly Peare, on the 12th March 1819, by me, Edwd Burke, Vicar

Joseph Murphy and Mary Slater were married in Church, by license, this 9th day of May 1819, by me, Edwd Burke, Vicar
Jno. Steadman

John Raine & Hannah McCane were married by me, after banns duly published, this 3rd day of June 1819, Edwd Burke, Vicar
Jno. Steadman

William Seeds and Bridget Fineran were married by me, (by license), this seventeenth day of June 1819, Edwd Burke, Vicar
John Steadman

[Page] 30

16th March 1819, baptized Anthony French son of John & Margaret Moore of Galway, J. Whitley

August 13th, Martin O'Toole & Rosa[mund] Kelly were married by me, (by license), this 13th day of Augt 1819, Edwd Burke, Vicar
Jno. Steadman

1819 August 22, baptized Louisa Wilhelmina Firth, Jas Daly

August 23, baptized George Brown, James Daly

September 27th, William Davis and Mary Rippingham were married by me, after banns duly published, this 27th day of September 1819, Edwd Burke, Vicar

John O'Callaghan bachelor & Honoria Bouch[is] widow were married by license, in this Church, October 24 1819, James Daly
Witness James Behun, Jno. Steadman

[Page] 31

November 10th 1819, baptized Jane Maria Dickinson
Do 14th, baptized William Swan, James Daly
Do 14th, baptized James Macartney, James Daly
Do 17th, baptized Thos Bell, James Daly
James Forster & Frances Ormsby, both of this Parish, were married in this Church, by license from the Warden of Galway, on the 11th of

December 1819, by me, James Daly
Witness: Andw Rud, Oliver Ormsby
Thomas Butler and Bridgett Tirrel, both of this Parish, were married by banns, in this Church, on the 20th day of December 1819, by me, Danl Foley
George Ryan baptized, on the 2nd January in the year of our Lord 1820, by me, James Daly
Patrick Duffy & Margaret Lally were married by license from the Archbishop of Tuam, on the 13th of January 1820, in this Church, by me, James Daly
Jno. Steadman
Willm Hodson to Catharine Scorry, both 77th Regt, by license from Archbishop of Tuam, Jany 17th 1820, J. Whitley, G[arriso]n Chapl[ain]
Jno. Steadman
Jany 21st 1820, James Prido to Catharine Manion by banns, J. Whitley
Jany 31st 1821, David [M?]arget to Margaret Groonet by banns, J. Whitley, G[arriso]n Ch[aplain]

[Page] 32

John Hacket & Maria McCullogh were married by license from the Archbishop of Tuam, January 30 1820, by me, James Daly
Jno. Steadman   Witness Andw Rud
December 1 1819, baptized Maria Wilson daughter to Mr Wilson of Arran, James Daly
March the 3rd 1820, Richard Roberts & Anne Holland were married by license, in the church of Galway, by me, James Daly
Witness John Holleran,   Jno. Steadman
April 4th 1820, William Carter and Margaret Warren were married by banns duly published, in the Parish Church of Galway, by me, Danl Foley for J. Whitley, Gar[riso]n Chap[lai]n
Jno. Steadman
Baptized Ellen Wheeler, April 14th 1820, James Daly
Daniel Considine & Honora King were married after banns duly published, on Wednesday the 26th of April 1820, by me, James Daly
Witness Jno. Steadman

[Page] 33

May 1st 1820, married John Pigott to Maria Hamilton, both of the 9th Veteran Bat[tall]ion, by publication [of banns], J. Whitley, G[arriso]n Chap[lai]n

Married May 1st 1820, James Crowe to Catherine Anderson of the 77th Foot, by publication [of banns], J. Whitley [The name Croughan is written above the name Crowe in a different hand and ink. In the index the entry appears under Croughan].

June 4th 1820, married Michael Tracy to Anne Ormsby, H. Morgan
Witness Oliver Ormsby

June 5 1820, William Halloran & Catharine Barry after banns duly published, were married, by me, James Daly
Jno. Steadman

July 3rd 1820, married John Regan to Margarette Cooke, by me, H. Morgan

June 14 1820, buried Mrs Cameron wife to Duncan Cameron, late Tide Surveyor, James Daly [This entry is in pencil and in a different hand to previous entries on the page].

[Page] 34

Roger Henigan married to Bridget Rogers, by me, Henry Morgan, July 5th 1820
Jno. Steadman

July 2nd, baptized John Smith, H. Morgan

July 8th 1820, Richard Lynch & Judith Burke were married by license from the Archbishop of Tuam, by me, James Daly
Witness Jno. Steadman

July 11 1820, Thos Sexton & Margaret O'Brien were married after banns duly published, by me, James Daly
Witness John Steadman

July 27th 1820, Thomas Broad and Bridget Mannin married (banns being duly published duly), by me, H. Morgan

John Joseph son of John & Margaret Moore, 16th July 1821, J. Whitley

[Page] 35

August 31 1820, married Daniel Foley & Elizabeth Browne by license from the Archbishop of Tuam
Witness Jno. Steadman   James Daly, Minister
August 31 1820, baptized Anne Dix, James Daly
Henrietta Eyre daughter of George & Ded Mar. Wilhel Maunsell[39] otherwise [von]hardenburg, his wife, Septr 2nd 1820, J. Whitley
Novr 19 1820, married John Browne of Demerera to Frances Clarke of the town of Galway, by license from Archbishop of Tuam, H. Morgan, Minister
Witness J. H. Browne, Jno. Steadman
Jany 24 1821, James Byrne & Eliza O'Hara were married by license from Tuam, by me, James Daly
Witness Const O'Hara, Jno. Steadman
February 4 1825, Henry Townsend & Celia Dwyer alias Nolan, were married by license from Tuam, by me, James Daly
Witness Wm Power

[Page] 36

February 8th 1821, bapd Jas Robinson, James Daly
February the 22nd 1821, Oliver Ormsby and Eliza Fitzsimons were married by license from Tuam, by me, John D'Arcy 1821
Witness present: Jno. Steadman
February the 24 1821, bapd Hubert Mannion, J. D'Arcy
Do the 26th 1821, bapd Elizabeth Morphet, J. D'Arcy
Feby 18[21], baptized John Roony, John D'Arcy
Feby 1821, baptized Jane Dennis, H. Morgan
Feby 1821, baptized Catharine Wheeler, H. Morgan
Decmr 4th 1821, Octavises son of Octavises & Harriet Carey, Lt Col 57th Reg, baptized, J. Whitley
March 13 1821, baptized Robert Langly, Jas Daly
April 1st, baptized Edward Caddy, J. D'Arcy

---

[39] Maria Wilhelmina Frederica von Hardenburgh married George Maunsell, brother of the Rev. E. E. Maunsell, see *Burke's Landed Gentry of Great Britain and Ireland* (1886).

May 21 1821, married Henry Stewart & Catherine Dillon, after banns duly published, in the Parish Church, James Daly
Witness Jno. Steadman
Baptized John & Michael Parish foundlings
26 May, baptized Margaret Waters, John D'Arcy
[28?] Do, baptized John French Gill, John D'Arcy

[Page] 37

May 28th, baptized Thomas Edward Flannery, John D'Arcy
June 4th, baptized Sarah Belinda Burton, John D'Arcy
June 17th, baptized John Kilroy, John D'Arcy
June 21, married by licence from Tuam, Henry Chalkner to Bridget Glynn, John D'Arcy
Witness Jno. Steadman
June 13th 1821, baptized Emily Pamalle Cashell
June 24th, Margarette Williams and Mary Anne Garrette, H. Morgan
August 12th 1820, baptized David Mitchel, H. Morgan
July 22nd 1821, baptized Maria Mitchel, H. Morgan
Augt 18 1821, married by license, Thomas J. A. Mullins and Eliza J. Blake, H. Morgan

[Page] 38

John Mills and Anne Geherty married, after banns duly published by me, this 23rd of July 1821, H. Morgan
Witness Jno. Steadman
July the 1st, baptized Mary Anne West, John D'Arcy
July the 1st 1821, baptized John Ford, J. D'Arcy
Do do 1821, received Margaret Ford having been previously baptized, J. D'Arcy
Do do 1821, baptized Harriet Hare, J. D'Arcy
Do do 1821, baptized Sarah Eames, John D'Arcy
Married by banns, George Carpenter & Elenor Sweeney, John D'Arcy, July the 24 1821
Present: Jno. Steadman
August 19 1821, married by license David Bynan seaman & Mary MacDannel, James Daly

August 28th 1821, married by license, William Swords & Catherine Sweeny, James Daly
Witness James Byrne
August 28th 1821, baptized John son of Major Browne, James Daly

[Page] 39

October 5th 1821, married by license, Mark Thomas of Sallyhill & Jane Seymour Dodsworth of Eyrecourt, by me, James Daly
Witness Geo. Symmers
October 10, baptized Laurence Kenny, John D'Arcy
October 23rd 1821, married John Reilly & Jane Davis after banns duly published, James Daly
October the 21, baptized Thomas Mcana[40], John D'Arcy
Do 28, baptized Simon Jude a Parish child, John D'Arcy
December 22nd, baptized Maria Edington, James Daly
Do 27th, married by banns, Samuel Graham & Mary Lydon, John D'Arcy   Witness Jno. Steadman
Dec 28th, baptized Elizabeth Clarke, John D'Arcy
January 13 1822, baptized Elisha Burns, J. D'Arcy
July 29th 1822, baptized Dunlop son of Digby Devenish of Arran, James Daly
July 30 1822, baptized Robert Burke son of James H. Burke of St Clerans & Anne his wife, James Daly, Warden

[Page] 40

Thos Fisher and Catherine Hopkins, widow, were married by me, September 13th 1819, Danl Foley for J. Whitley, G[arriso]n Chaplain
Sept 12 1820, baptized John Heatly Frith, James Daly
July 12th 1821, baptized Catharine Wheeler, James Daly
Baptized Richard Sadlier son of Wm and Mary Sadlier, Feb 24 1822, H. Morgan, 57th Regt
[The Rev Henry Morgan baptized the children in the following 4 entries for Rev John Whitley, Garrison Chaplain. Rev J. Whitley later signed each entry to verify it].

---

[40] 'vide George' in index.

Baptized Robert Carey, son of Colonel Carey, 57th Regt[41], Jan 20th 1822, signed H. Morgan for Revd John Whitley, J. Whitley

Baptized William Curry son of James & Mary Curry, 57th Regt, Feb 18th 1822, for John Whitley, J. Whitley, G[arrison] C[haplain], H. Morgan

Baptized Sarah Cox, Febr 13th 1822, daughter of Danl & Catharine Cox, 57th Regt, for John Whitley, J. Whitley, H. Morgan

Baptized William son of Stephen and Sarah Thompson, 57th Regt, H. Morgan for J. Whitley, Febr 24 1822, J. Whitley, G[arrison] C[haplain] [42]

[Page] 41

Married Thomas Heavy to Catharine Loftus, by licence from the Archbishop of Tuam, Febr 26th 1822, H. Morgan

Married John Harrison to Jane McDonald, by licence from the Archbishop of Tuam, March 9th 1822, H. Morgan, Vicar

Baptized Joseph Mortimer, March 9th 1822, H. Morgan, Vicar

April 14, baptized Richard Hedges Eyre Maunsell, John D'Arcy

May the 3rd, baptized Henry Farrington, J. D'Arcy

May the 19th, baptized Thomas Shedrake, J. D'Arcy

Do do, a foundling by name John, J. D'Arcy

June 5 1822, baptized Joseph Edward Dickinson, James Daly

March 13 1822, baptized Eliza Compton

June 19 1822, married John Kelly & Anne Currie, James Daly Jno. Steadman

June 31st, baptized Charles George Frith, J. D'Arcy

[Page] 42

July 23rd 1822, baptized Eliza Robinson daughter of Wm Robinson, of the 43rd Foot, Thos Coffey

July 28th 1822, baptized Anne Marlow daughter of James Marlow, of the 43rd Foot, Thos Coffey

---

[41] 57th Regt appears twice.
[42] The date Decr 11th 1820 appears above this entry.

Augt 12th 1822, baptized Antony Saver son of [blank] Saver, of the Police Establishment, Thos Coffey
Augt 18th 1822, baptized Joseph Frith, H. Morgan
Augt 14, baptized William Alexander Ryan, J. D'Arcy
Do 11th, baptized Mary Ann Middleton, J. D'Arcy
August 28th, married by licence from the Archbishop of Tuam, Henry Browne Esqr to Maria Madden, spinster of this Parish, John D'Arcy Witness: Geo [Atkins], Jno. Steadman
September 15th, baptized Dora Calcut, John D'Arcy
October 4th 1822, Roger Black of the 3rd R[egiment] Veterans & Elizabeth Nislor were married in this Church, by me, James Daly Witness Thomas Driscoll
Baptized Henrietta Cashell, December 16 1822, James Daly

[Page] 43

Married Martin Geraghty to Mary Taffe, after banns duly published, by the Revd John Whitley, Garrison Chaplain, Novr 2nd 1822, H. Morgan, Vicar
Married John Lyons to Catharine Barry after banns duly published, by the Revd John Whitley, Garrison Chaplain, Novr 10th 1822, H. Morgan, Vicar
Married James Madigan to Mary Bourke, after banns duly published, by the Revd John Whitley, Garrison Chaplain, Decr 2nd 1822, H. Morgan
Married John Carter to Mary Rachars, by licence from the Archbishop of Tuam, by the Rev John Whitley, Garrison Chaplain, Decr 2nd 1822, H. Morgan, Vicar
Baptized Margarette Dix, Nov 11th 1822, H. Morgan
Baptized William Grey, Novr 24th 1822, H. Morgan
Baptized James Daniel, Decr 8th 1822, H. Morgan
Baptized Margaret Garret, Jany 19 1823, J. D'Arcy
Married William Mandie 3rd of the Invalid Artillery to Honora Connell, by publication, Jany 20th 1823, J. Whitley, G[arrison] C[haplain]

[Page] 44

Married by licence from the Archbishop of Tuam, James Blake of Invern Lodge to Helen Burke of Dominick Street, Galway, spinster, H. Morgan, Vicar, Jany 24th 1823
Witnesses present Jno. Steadman, Henry Cox, John Cady, Mary Cox
Married by licence from the Archbishop of Tuam, Eneas Coghlan to Cecily McDonough, H. Morgan, Vicar, Feby 5th 1823
Witness present Henry Cox, Eneas Coughlan
Feby 23 1823, baptized Catharine Swan daughter of Richard Swan, H. Morgan, Vicar
March 12th 1823, baptized Mary Parker daughter of James Parker, H. Morgan, Vicar

[Page] 45

March 1823, baptized Susanah daughter of Oliver Ormsby of the town of Galway, H. Morgan, Vicar
April 5th 1823, baptized Henry son of John Thomas, Sergeant of the 3rd Vet. Battalion, H. Morgan, Vicar
Thursday April 17th 1823, Harloe Dennis Esq. & Miss Jane Bloomfie[l]d were married by licence from the Archbishop of Tuam, by me, James Daly
Witness Harloe Irwin, J. Bloomfield, W. W. Bloomfield, H. Morgan
Monday April 7 1823, Henry Bright was married to Jane Heath alias Powel, by licence from the Archbishop of the Tuam, by me, H. Morgan [After Bright the words 'to Jane Powel alias Heath' have been scored out].
Married this day by licence from the Archbishop of Tuam, James Foster of Clifden to Mary Ann Osberne, March the 30 1823, John D'Arcy, Minister
Present: Jno. Steadman

[Page] 46

Sunday April 20 1823, baptized Elizabeth Burdish daughter of John Burdish, soldier of the 3rd Royal Vetn Batn, H. Morgan

April 30th 1823, Peter St John Conolly, printer & Ellen Palmer, spinster, were married after banns duly published, by me, James Daly, Warden
Witness Jno. Steadman
May the 5th 1823, Charles John Lynch of the city of Stockholm and Anne McMullen of the Parish of St Nicholas, Galway, were married after banns duly published, by me, Henry Morgan, Vicr
Witness Jno. Steadman
May 18 1823, Michael Morton was married to Eliza Gardener, spinster, after banns duly published, by me, H. Morgan, Vicar
Witness Jno. Steadman
Baptized Sarah Maria Cuppaidge, on 29th day of April 1823 three, John D'Arcy
May 11, baptized Catherine Manning, J. D'Arcy

[Page] 47

May 19 1823, Thomas Mahon and Jane Blake, spinster, were married by licence from the Archbishop of Tuam, by me, H. Morgan, Vicar
Witness Henry Blake, Edmd Mahon, James Blake, Thomas Blake
June 8th 1823, William Sheppard and Margarette Burke alias McCarthy, widow, were married by licence from the Archbishop of Tuam, by me, H. Morgan, Vicar
Jno. Steadman
June 1st 1823, Charles Walsh son of [blank] Walsh of the Parish of St Nicholas, was baptized by the Revd John Whitley, H. Morgan, Vicar
June 14th 1823, George Bently and Margarette Colles otherwise Joyce, widow, were married by licence from the Archbishop of Tuam, by me, H. Morgan, Vicr
Witness Jno. Steadman
June 15, baptized Samuel Shaw, J. D'Arcy
July 21st, baptized Catherine Maria Darcy daughter of Major Darcy, 37 Regt, J. D'Arcy

[Page] 48

Thomas Trins, Private Soldier of the 3rd Vet. Battallion and Mary O'Brien, spinster of the Parish of St Nicholas, Galway, were married

60

after banns duly published, by me, H. Morgan, Vicar, for the Revd John Whitley, Garrison Chaplain, July 28th 1823

August 1st 1823 I baptized [blank – no entry follows]

August 11th 1823, William Kelly Wilton & Mary Martin were married by license from the Archbishop of Tuam, in the Parish Church of St Nicholas, Galway, by me, James Daly. Witness present: Anthony Martin, Thomas Martin, Henry Caddy, Wm Tayler D'Arcy

August 17th 1823, John Darcy & Maria Marshall were married by license from the Archbishop of Tuam, in the Parish Church of Galway, by me, James Daly

Witness present: J. Marshall, H. Marshall, Henry Caddy

[Page] 49

August 23rd 1823, Mr John Hopkins of Tuam & Maria Fitzimmons were married by licence from the Archbishop of Tuam, in this Church, by me, James Daly

Witness present: James Forster, Alex Lynch, Arthur Cartiatt, John Robert Fitzsimons

Baptized [blank] Bently daughter of George Bently, H. Morgan, Vicar, Augst 23rd 1823

Baptized August 20th 1823, Julia daughter of Wm & Margaret Fitzpatrick 3rd Vetn Battalion, J. Whitley, G[arrison] C[haplain]

Sept 1st 1823, John son of Sergeant John & Grace Platt, 3rd Vetn Battalion, J. Whitley

Jany 12th 1823, Margaret daughter of John & Elinor Barlow, 3rd Vetn Battalion, H. Morgan

June 1823, baptized Edward Joseph son of Reuben and [blank] Hughes, born 5th of June 1823, baptized sometime in same month, Edwd Burke, Vicar

August the 9th, baptized Margaret Wheeler, J. D'Arcy

[Page] 50

September 30th, baptized Barry Harcourt Mortimer, J. D'Arcy

September 11th 1823, baptized Hariette Blakney [sic] daughter of John Henry Blakeney of Abbert, H. Morgan, Vicar

Married this day by banns, James Glynn, weaver to Eleanour Connolly, widow, both of this Parish, John D'Arcy
Present: Jno. Steadman
Baptized John Doe, this day September 14 1823, J. D'Arcy
Baptized Sepr 16th 1823, Henry Galway son of Daniel and Mary Kirby, 3rd Vetn Battal[io]n, J. Whitley, G[arrison] C[haplain]
Septr 22nd 1823, Andrew Rankin and Mary Griffin were married by license from the Archbishop of Tuam, in the Parish Church of St Nicholas, Galway, by me, Edwd Burke, Vicar
Witness present: Jno. Steadman

[Page] 51

Octr 30th 1823, baptized Susanna daughter of Roger & Mary Black, 3rd Vetn Batn, J. Whitley, G[arrison] C[haplain]
Novr 3rd 1823, baptized Wm [Hassit] son of Wm [Hassit] and Ann Yellon, 3rd Vetn Battal[io]n, J. Whitley, G[arrison] C[haplain]
December 29, baptized Margaret Pard,[43] John D'Arcy
Jany 11 1824, baptized Cynis Butler son of William Butler of Galway, H. Morgan
Married after banns duly published, John How, marine on board His Majesty's brig of war *Plumper* to Bridget Kealy, spinster, by me, H. Morgan, Vicar, Jan 19th 1824
Jan 25th 1824, baptized Richard Matthew Peare son of Richard Peare and Andrew Kirwan Flannery son of Michael Flannery, H. Morgan, Vicar
October 1827, baptized Frederich Buxton D'Alton son to Lieutenant Dalton [sic] of the Water Guard, James Daly

[Page] 52

Married Decemr 15th 1823, Wm Wilson, 3rd Vetn Battn to Kitty O'Sullivan, by publication of banns, J. Whitley, G[arrison] C[haplain][44]
Married Decemr 22nd 1823, Hugh Reed, 3rd Vet. Battn to Harriet Williams, by banns, by J. Whitley, G[arrison] C[haplain]

---

[43] 'Supplier, Dominick St' is recorded in the index.
[44] J. Whitley, G[arrison] C[haplain] appears twice

John Taylor and Bridget McGrath, spinster of this Parish, were married in the Church of St Nicholas, after banns duly published, by me, H. Morgan, Vicar, Jan 26 1824

February 3rd 1824, Michael Francis Geoghehan & Mary Sutherland were married by licence from Tuam, in this Church, by me, James Daly

Witness present: John Sutherland, Jno. O'Brien

Feb the 1st, baptized Isabella Joynt, J. D'Arcy

Feby 8th 1824, baptized Bridget daughter of Henry Bright, H. Morgan

F[ebruary] 8th 1824, baptized John Harkins Carrique Moran son of John Moran, H. Morgan

Baptized Charles son of James Compton of Oranmore, H. Morgan

March [?] 1824, baptized Henry Caddy, John D'Arcy

March 12, baptized James Miles Townsend Reeley son of J. L.Reeley Esq. of West House[45], John D'Arcy [This entry inserted later in a different ink]

[Page] 53

March the 12th, baptized John Dickinson, John D'Arcy

March 22nd, baptized Mary daughter of James & Mary Smith, 1st Vetn Battn, J. Whitley, G[arrison] C[haplain]

March 29th, baptized Susanna daughter of Isaack & Susanna Farrel, 1st Vet. Battn, J. Whitley

Apr 17th 1824, baptized Arariaita Bloomfield Dennis daughter of Lieutenant Harlow Dennis [J.P.], late 101st Regt Foot, H. Morgan, Vicr

April 25, baptized Sarah Williams, John D'Arcy

April 5th, baptized at Oranmore, Charles Francis Allen son to the Police Constable, James Daly

May 2nd 1824, baptized William Mannen, John D'Arcy

Do 4th, baptized Martha Kenny, John D'Arcy

Do do, baptized John Macarthy, J. D'Arcy

June 7th 1824, baptized Joseph son of Joseph & Elizabeth Simmonds, 1st Vetn Battn, J. Whitley

---

[45] The index of the register refers to J.L. Reeley of Scarva House, Co Down and West House, Galway.

June the 14 1824, married this day by bans duly published, Simon Peters, a mariner from the coast of Guine[a] & Margaret Geraghty, spinster of this Parish, John D'Arcy
Present: Jno. Steadman

[Page] 54

June the 15 1824, married by bans this day, Michael O'Reilly and Mary Ford, both of this Parish, John D'Arcy
Present: Jno. Steadman
June 4th 1824, baptized John Cannon French, J. Daly
July 10th 1824, Benjamin Rollin, policeman and Margaret Kelly of Oranmore, were married by license from Tuam, in this Church, by me, James Daly
[Witness] Edwd Howard, Jno. Steadman
July 11th 1824, Mr William Stephens of Newcastle Brewery and Catharine Ryan, spinster of Galway, were married by licence from Tuam, in the Collegiate Church of St Nicholas, by me, James Daly
Witness [Jno.] C. ffrench, Jno. Steadman
July 6th 1824, baptized for Mr Whitly, Mary Anne daughter of James and Mary Oakes, of the 1st Veteran Battalion, James Daly
July the 27th, baptized Frances Reilly, John D'Arcy

[Page] 55

August 16th 1824, Lieut Edmond Mahon, half pay 70th Foot and Jane Davies of Galway, daughter of the late Michael Davies of Hamstead Esqr in this county, were married by license from the Archbishop of Tuam, in the Collegiate Church of St Nicholas, by me, H. Morgan, Vicr
Witness: Lambart Mahon, Rich. Oct[avius?] Morgan, Jno. Steadman
August 22, baptized Robert Logun, John D'Arcy
Do do, baptized Mary McDonough, J. D'Arcy
November 19th 1824, James Beatty, policeman & Bridget Carrick of Oranmore, were married by license from Tuam, by me, James Daly
Witness present: Grey [sic] Beatty, Jno. Steadman
1824, baptized William Cork, Novembr the 16th, J. D'Arcy
1824, baptized Henry Taylor, November the 21st, J. D'Arcy

1824, baptized James Maxwell, Novermber the 28th, H. Morgan, Vicr
1824 Decr 6th, Patrick Graghane and Anne Foy were married after banns duly published, by me, H. Morgan, Vicr
Decr 28th 1824, James Murray & Mary Anne Forbes were married in this Church after banns duly published, by me, James Daly
Witness present George Wheeler, David Smyth, John Cullen

[Page] 56

January 29 1825, Mr Henry Benton & Mary Topham, spi[nster], both of this Parish, were married by license from Tuam, in this Church, by me, James Daly, Warden of Galway
Witness present David Smyth, Jno. Steadman
Married this day by bans duly published, Michael Martyn & Mary Reilly, both of this Parish, John D'Arcy February 7th 1825
February 8th 1825, Charles Smyth & Anne Keatinge, both of this Parish, were married after banns duly published, in this Church, by me, James Daly
Witness present John Wheeler, Henry Caddy
February 8th 1825, baptized David Smyth son of Charles & Anne, James Daly
Feby 11th 1825, [Callin] Dow and Catherine Cullin, both of this Parish, were married by license from Tuam, in this Church, by me, Edwd Burke
Witness present: Jno. Steadman
Baptized David son of Thos & Jane Boland, March 4th 1825, J. Whitley
11th April 1825, Benjn son of James and Mary Aspin, 3rd Vetn Batt., J. Whitley

[Page] 57

Feby 14 1825, William Satliffe and Mary Whelan, widow, both of the Parish of St Nicholas, were married after banns duly published, by me, H. Morgan, Vicar
Feby 28th 1825, James Strachan, mariner and Ellen Conway, both of this Parish, also Owen Deace and Mary Higgins, both of this Parish,

were married in this Church after banns duly published, by me, H. Morgan, Vicr
Witness present: Jno. Steadman
April 4 1825, married by bans duly published, Patrick Mellain & Eleanner Gunning, both of this Parish, John D'Arcy
March the 1st 1825, I baptized Honor Burdge daughter to Mr Burdge, watchmaker of this town, J. Daly
April 21st, married this day by licence from the court of Tuam, Thomas Maxwell & Sarah Gavin, both of this Parish, John D'Arcy
Jno. Steadman

[Page] 58

April 25th 1825, John Barnard of her Majesty's brig *Plumper* & Elizabeth White, spinster of this Parish, having license from Tuam, were married in the church of Galway, by me, James Daly, Warden
Witness present Wm Hutchinson, J. Henry Doyle
April 28th 1825, baptized William Thomas son of William Kelly Wilton, James Daly
May 11th 1825, Toby Butler & Mary Browne, both of this Parish, were married after banns duly published, in this Church, by me, James Daly
Witness Jno. Steadman
April 28th 1825, baptized Eliza Kavars, James Daly
Octob[er] 6th 1825, baptized Sarah Matilda Coffey daughter of Revd Thos Coffey and Susanna his wife, born Augt 25th 1825, Thos Coffey
May 22nd 1825, baptized George Wheeler son John & Margt Wheeler, born 12th May 1825, Edwd Burke, Vicar
May 11th 1825, baptized Thomas Henry Mahon son to Major Mahon of Belleville, James Daly, Warden of Galway
June the 3rd 1825, baptized Elizabeth Stephens daughter of William Bastable & Kitty Stephens, James Daly, Warden

[Page] 59

June 6th 1825, baptized William Mannion son to Mr Mannion, dancing master, James Daly, Warden of Galway
June 16th 1825, married by license from the A[rch]bishop of Tuam, Montgomery Moore and Mary Whitley, J. Whitley

Baptized Robert son Wm Barr and Mary Do, 1st Vet. Battn, J. Whitley, G[arrsion] C[haplain]
August the 14th 1825, I baptized Margaret O'Hara second daughter to James O'Hara Junior of West Lodge & Anne his wife, James Daly, Warden of Galway [pencil annotations in margin working out her age in 1856 as 31]
August 14, married this day by bans duly published, Hugh Comber & Catherine Prendergast, both residing in this Parish, John D'Arcy
May the 9th 1827, baptized Jane Stephens daughter to William Bastabell & Kitty Stephens, James Daly, Warden of Galway

[Page] 60

August 15th 1825, Wm son of Jas & Mary Oakes, 1st Vetn Battn, J. Whitley
John son of Joseph & Elizabeth Symmond, 1st Vetn Battn, J. Whitley
September the 21st 1825, I baptized Georgina Martin daughter to Anthony Martin Esq. of Dangan, James Daly, Warden of Galway
August 24 1825, baptized Georgina daughter of Anthony Martin Esqr of Dangan, James Daly
Baptized Octr 15th 1825, Edward son of Edward & Elizabeth Guest, 1st R[oya]l Vett. Battn
William son of Mathew & Catharine Hickie, 1st R[oya]l Vet. Batt., J. Whitley, G[arrison] C[haplain]
April 1824, baptized Henry Robert Cashel son to Mr Cashel, Inspector of Galway Fisheries, James Daly, Warden of Galway
October the 18th 1825, baptized Jane daughter to Henry Bright, nailer of the town of Galway, James Daly, Warden of Galway

[Page] 61

November the 1st 1825, baptized Elizabeth daughter of Mr Middleton, the cooperer of Spanish Parade, Galway, James Daly, Warden of Galway
Novr 7, married by banns duly published, this 7th day of November 1825, John Jackson & Mary King, both of this Parish, John D'Arcy Present: Jno. Steadman
Novembr 9th, received into the Church by public baptism, he having

been before privately baptized, William [Land] Hutchinson Carr son of Capt Hutchinson of His Majesty's brigg *Plumper,* aged three years, John D'Arcy

4th Decemr 1825, baptized Charles son of Thos Kimmoth & Jane his wife, 1st Vet. Battn, J. Whitley, G[arrison] C[haplain]

Jany 10 1826, Dorcas daughter of Thomas Smith, of the Constabularly Police, was baptized by me, at Oranmore, H. Morgan

Jany 25th 1826, bapd Robert son of Robert & Sarah Bowles, 1st Vet. Battn, J. Whitley

1826 January, baptized Margaret Eleanour Laurence daughter of W. Laurence Esq. of Bellview, John D'Arcy

[Page] 62

February the 6th 1826, William Anderson & Rachel Topham were married by licence from Tuam, in this Church, by me, James Daly, Warden of Galway

Witness present: James Huston, D. Murray, Jno. Steadman

February the 6th 1826, Jhon [sic] Thompson of Westport & Mary Britton alias Monaghan, of Ballinrobe, were married by license from Tuam, in the Collegiate Church of Galway, by me, James Daly, Warden of Galway

Witness present: Jno. Steadman

February the 9th 1826, Michael Browne Esq. & Harriett alias Deborah McDonough, were married after license had from the Archbishop of Tuam, in the Collegiate Church of Galway, by me, James Daly, Warden of Galway

Witness present: Robt Martin, J. Lushington Reilly, Nicholas Browne, Th[os] A. Poppleton

[Page] 63

Baptized Misiah Butler

1826 Feby 21st, the Very Revd James Daly, Warden of Galway and Jemima Browne, spinster, were married after licence had from the Archbishop of Tuam, in the Collegiate Church of Galway, by me, Danl Foley

Witness present: John Steadman

Feby 20 1826, baptized William son of Thomas Black, of the Constabulary Police at Oranmore, born Feby 18, H. Morgan, Vicr

March 1st 1826, baptized Frederick Simpson Grey, born Feby 12th 1826, son of Doctor Robert Rogers Grey, H. Morgan

March 7th 1827, John Fowler, Royal Marine of his Majesty's Brig of War *Plumper* and Bridget Butler otherwise Fyrrall, were married in the Parish Church of St Nicholas, after banns duly published, by me, H. Morgan, Vicr

Jno. Steadman

April the 9th 1826, James Cudden & Rebecca Molowny were married by license from Tuam, in the Collegiate Church of St Nicholas, by me, James Daly, Warden of Galway

Witness present: Timothy Larklin, Jno. Steadman

[Page] 64

March 7th 1826, baptized Catharine daughter of Wm & Ellen Merchant, 1st R[oya]l Vet. Battn, J. Whitley & Elizabeth son [sic] of Hugh & Elizth Bird, 1st R[oyal] V[eteran] Bn, J. Whitley

Baptized April 3rd 1826, Joseph son of Joseph & Mary [Bu]tton, 1st R[oya]l V[eteran] Batt., J. Whitley

April the 9th 1826, Jno. Logan son of Mr Logan, the surveyor, was baptized by me, James Daly, Warden of Galway

Baptized April 9th 1826, Emily Mary Cathne daughter of Thos Henry Doyle, Adjutnt 1st Roy[a]l Vetn Batt. and Jemma Anne his wife, J. Whitley

April 2nd 1826, William son of Tomkins and Jane Brew of Applevale in the County of Clare, was baptized by me, at the Police Barrack in Oranmore, born March 14th 1826, H. Morgan, Vicr

April 8th 1826, Bridget daughter of John and Bridget Ryan was baptized by me, born 18th [blank], H. Morgan, Vicr

April 13th, George Morgan Franklin son of Lieutenant Robert Franklin and Susan Franklin was baptized by me, born April 4th, H. Morgan, Vicr

April 24 1826, married by licence John De[nis] & Ellen Dignan of this Parish, John D'Arcy

Present Thos E. Langley

[Page] 65

April 19th 1826, baptized Henry son of James and Mary Compton of Oranmore, born April 6th, H. Morgan

May 15th 1826, Patrick Hearnan and Mary Higgins, spinster, both of this Parish, were married after banns duly published, in the Parish Church of St Nicholas, by me, H. Morgan, Vicar

May 21 1826, baptized John Mullins, John D'Arcy

June 11th, baptized John Bloomfield Denis, John D'Arcy

June 14th 1826, baptized Essy daughter of Henry and Lucy Carr, (born April 20th 1826), H. Morgan, Vicar

July 16 1826, Richard son of John Massy, Private Soldier of the 22nd Regt [of] Foot and Anne his wife, was baptized in the Parish Church of St Nicholas, by me, H. Morgan, Vicr for Rev. J. Whitley, G[arrison] C[haplain], born July 6th 1826

July 23rd 1826, John son of Thomas Perry, Private Soldier of the 22nd Regt [of] Foot and Catharine his wife, born on the 14th of May, was baptized in the Parish Church of St Nicholas, by me, H. Morgan, Vicr, for Revd J. Whitley, G[arrison] C[haplain]

July 27 1826, baptized William son of Jas Beatty, policeman & Bridget his wife, James Daly, Warden

[Page] 66

John Flury, Private Soldier of His Majesty's 22nd Regt of Foot and Catharine Birmingham, (spinster) of this Parish, were married in the Parish Church of St Nicholas, after banns duly published, by me, H. Morgan, Vicr, July 31st 1826, for the Revd J. Whitley, G[arrison] C[haplain]

August 6 1826, baptized Ann Bruce, J. D'Arcy

August 6, baptized William Walton Kenny, J. D'Arcy

August 13, baptized Charlotte Moore Reilly, J. D'Arcy

August 16, married by banns duly published, William Edmunds & Ann Handcock alias Robinson, both of this Parish, J. D'Arcy

Witness Jno. Steadman

September the 3rd 1826, Mr James Keogh of Galway & Maria Boyle, spinster, were married (after license had from Tuam), in the Collegiate Church of Galway, by me, James Daly, Warden of Galway
Witness present James Bayley, Jno. Steadman

[Page] 67

August 20th 1826, baptized Fardy son of John Callinan and Margarette his wife, born August 13th, H. Morgan, Vicar
August 13th 1826, George Binns and Catherine Higgins, spinster, both of this Parish, were married by license from the Archbishop of Tuam, by me, H. Morgan, Vicar
September 10th 1826, Phillip Dwyer of the Parish of Rahoon and Honour Shannen, spinster of the Parish of Oranmore, were married by license from the Archbishop of Tuam, in the Parish Church of St Nicholas, by me, H. Morgan, Vicar
September the 10th 1826, I baptized Sarah Persse daughter to Burton Persse of Persse Lodge & Martha his wife, James Daly, Warden of Galway
Nelson Cornvill, Private Soldier & drummer in His Majesty's 22nd Regt of Foot and Anne McGanley, spinster of Portumna, were married after banns duly published, by me, H. Morgan, Vicar, September 13th 1826

[Page] 68

December 28th 1821, Joseph son of Oliver Ormsby and Elizabeth his wife, was baptized by me, H. Morgan, born Decr 18 1821
October the 9th 1826, John Green & Maria Lackey, both of this Parish, were married by license from Tuam, with the consent of parents & guardians, in the Collegiate Church of Galway, by me, James Daly, Warden of Galway
Witness present Patk King, Pat Furry
Bedilia Charlotte, born September 24th 1826, daughter of David and Ann Mitchelle was baptized by me, on the 5th of October 1826, H. Morgan
Thomas, born September 13th 1826, son of Thomas and Jane Chester, baptized Sept 15th 1826, by me, H. Morgan, Vicar

November the 17th 1826, baptized in the Parish of Rahoone, Joseph Lally son of Margaret & John, James Daly, Warden of Galway

[Page] 69

Novr 17 1826, baptized George John son of George McCarty and Sarah his wife, born Nov 10 1826, H. Morgan, Vicar
[the following entry is all crossed out] Jan 23rd 1827, John Burke of Waterford and Elizabeth Johnson, spinster of this Parish, were marrried after banns duly published, in the Parish Church of St Nicholas, by me, H. Morgan, Vicar
Anna Maria, born Feby 16 1827, daughter of Thomas Butler of Winterfield in the County of Galway and of Elizabeth his wife, baptized March 16 1827, by me, H. Morgan, Vicar
Neil Edmonstone, born April 8th 1827, son of Lestock Francis Boilean, Lieutenant in the Royal Navy and of Charlotte his wife, was baptized April 28th 1827, by me, H. Morgan, Vicar
May the 10th 1827, Charles Vordun of the town of Galway & Charlotte Carter, spinster, were married by license, in the Collegiate Church of St Nicholas, by me, James Daly, Warden of Galway
Witness present   Saml Carter, Jno. Steadman
May the 5th 1827, christened Charles Drelincourt Campbell, he having been previously baptized in England, James Daly, Warden

[Page] 70

March 20th 1827, married John Dyas, 15th Regt of Foot to Elizabeth Burk, J. Whitley, G[arrison] C[haplain]
March 21, baptized John Meredith Atkinson, J. D'Arcy
Baptized August 6th 1826, Rebecca daughter of Edward & Frances Church, 22nd Regt of Foot, J. Whitley
June the 4th, baptized John Wheeler, John D'Arcy
June 13th [14th is crossed out] 1827, baptized Massy James son of Valentine Browne and Fanny Matilda his wife, born May 24 1827, H. Morgan, Vicr
June 14 1827, baptized Catharine daughter of Thomas Maxwell and Sarah his wife, born June 12th 1827, H. Morgan

June 16 1827, baptized James son of James Killery of Shantalla and Mary his wife, born May 28th 1827, H. Morgan

June 17th 1827, baptized Mary Anne daughter of David Woolner of the Water Guard and Mary Anne his wife, born May 19th 1827, H. Morgan

June 26th 1827, baptized John Maxwell son of John & Catharine, James Daly, Warden of Galway

[Page] 71

July 1st 1827, baptized George son of George Upfield, Private Soldier in His Majesty's 17th Regt of Foot and of Jane his wife, born June 23rd 1827, H. Morgan, Vicar

July 8th 1827, baptized Elizabeth Beasmore daughter of John Beasmore, Sergeant in the 17th Regt of Foot and of Sarah Jane his wife, born June 28th 1827, H. Morgan

August 5th 1827, baptized Sarah, daughter of Charles Smyth and Anna his wife, born July 30 1827, H. Morgan, Vicr

August 6 1827, baptized Martha Boyd daughter to Henry & Martha of the Water Guard

August 9th 1827, George Fox & Ellen Considine were married by license from Tuam, in the Collegiate Church of St Nicholas, by me, James Daly

Witness [blank]

[Page] 72

August 18th 1827, baptized Henry Blake Mahon son of Thomas Mahon of Bellville in the County of Galway and Jane his wife, born August 7th 1827, H. Morgan, Vicr

Septr 16 1827, baptized Margarette Anne daughter of James Crawford and Mary Anne his wife, born August 16th 1827, H. Morgan

November 24 1827, Walter Larkin and Rebecca Scanlan were married in the Collegiate Church after license had from Tuam, by me, James Daly

Witness Jno. C. Ffrench

Novr 24 1827, baptized Robert son of Henry Caddy and Mary his wife, born Novr 22 1827, H. Morgan, Vicr

September 3 1827, baptized Louisa daughter of Mr Burdge, watchmaker of this town, James Daly, Warden

[Page] 73

Decr 11 1827, William Albut and Margaret F[erg], spinster, were married after banns duly published, in the church of St Nicholas, by me, H. Morgan, Vicr

January the 1st 1828, Revd Henry Morgan & Ellen Davis, spinster, were married by license from Tuam, in the Collegiate Church of St Nicholas, by me, James Daly, Warden
Witness Alexr Symmers, Jno. Steadman

January 3 1828, Patrick Duane of Clifden & Eliza Devenish, spinster, were married by license from Tuam, in the Collegiate Church of St Nicholas, by me, James Daly, Warden

1828

Jany 6 1828, baptized George Johns son of George and Mary Johns of the Coast Guard, John D'Arcy

January 15 1828, John Burke of Moyglass in the County of Galway and Emily Frances Blake, spinster of Galway, were married by license from the Archbishop of Tuam, in the Parish Church of St Nicholas, by me, H. Morgan, Vicr

[Page] 74

January the 18th 1828, Thomas Mitchell of Dublin & Anne Tracy, (widow) of Galway, were married by license from Tuam, in the Collegiate Church of St Nicholas, by me, James Daly, Warden
Witness present John Reilly, Wm Freeland

February 19, baptized Ann Parker, John D'Arcy

March the 9th 1828, Walter Brandon of Galway and Mary Carty of Dominick St, were married by license from Tuam, in the Collegiate Church of St Nicholas, by me, James Daly
Witness present John Rooney, Henry Caddy

1828 March 13, married this day by the licence of the Archbishop of Tuam, John Tracy of the Nursery Company to Harriet Trimble of Cunnemara, John D'Arcy
Jno. Steadman

[Page] 75

March 16 1828, Jane daughter of George Johnstone, Private Soldier in His Majesty's 34th Regt of Foot, H. Morgan
March 23 1828, baptized Elizabeth Donnelly daughter [of] Connor Donnelly, mariner and Jane his wife, born March 20 1828, H. Morgan
March 23 1828, baptized Sarah daughter of James Chambers and Ellen his wife, born March 18 1828, H. Morgan
May 19 1828, baptized Rebecca Catharine daughter of Lieutenant Harlow Dennis H.P. [?], 101st Regt of Foot and of Jane his wife, born May 7th 1828, H. Morgan, Vicr
June 22 1828, baptized Mary daughter of John Carr of the Waterguard and Jane his wife, born on the 10th of June 1828, H. Morgan
June 23 1828, James McLoughlin and Mary Mulin were married after banns duly published, by me, James Daly, Warden of Galway

[Page] 76

June 15, baptized Mary Anne daughter of Thomas and Jane Chester of the 64th Regt, by Revd J. Whitley, Gar[rison] Chap[lain], signed H. Morgan, Vicr June 22 1828
June 23 1828, baptized Henry Brooke son of William Kelly Wilton of Ashley Park, Galway and Mary his wife, born June 3 1828, H. Morgan, Vicar
July 10 1828, John Hudley, Private Soldier of the 64th Regt and Anne Hopkins, spinster, were married in the Parish Church of St Nicholas, after banns duly published, by me, H. Morgan, Vicr
July 14, baptized William Wright son of [blank] Wright, soldier of the 64th Regiment, John D'Arcy
I baptized Martin Cavanagh son to M. Cavanagh of the 64th Regiment, James Daly, Warden [no date]

[Page] 77

October 8th 1828, baptized privately at Merlin Park, Charles 'son of Walter Laurence Esq. of Bellville' [crossed out] and also Ann his twin sister, daughter children [this word inserted later] of sd. W. Laurence of Bellville & Georgina his wife, John D'Arcy, Vicar

Eliza Johnstone daughter of James Kearney, Comptroller of the Customs, Galway and of Eliza his wife, baptized August 16 1828, born August 3rd, H. Morgan, Vicar

October 10 1828, John Costello, barrister at law of Dublin and Mary Blake, spinster of the town of Galway, were married by license from the Archbishop of Tuam, by me, H. Morgan, Vicar
Witness John Burke, J. B. Blake

Novr 2 1828, James son of Oliver Glanville of the Parish of Camborne, County of Cornwall, miner in the Tully lead mine and of Maria his wife baptized, born Septem. 25 1828, H. Morgan

Novr 12 1828, baptized John son of William Leath, drummer in his Majesty's 64th Regt of Foot and of Mary his wife, born Novr 2nd 1828, H. Morgan, Vicar for Rev. John Whitley, Garrison Chaplain

[Page] 78

Novr 19 1828, Wandell Allso[p], miner from the Tully mines, of the Parish of Wordsworth in Derbyshire and Mary Murry of the Parish of Ballynacourty, were married by license from the Archbishop of Tuam, by me, H. Morgan, Vicr
Witness Francis Morgan

October 20 1828, baptized William son of Alexander Hay of Villa, architect and of Eleanor his wife, born September 23 1828, H. Morgan, Vicr

November 30 1828, baptized Marian Frances daughter of the Revd Henry Morgan, Vicar of St Nicholas and of Eleanor his wife, born Nov 18 1828, H. Morgan, Vicr

Decr 21 1828, baptized Mary Jane daughter of Nicholas Burge of Galway, jeweller and of Louisa his wife, born Decr 2 1828, H. Morgan, Vicr

December 22 1828, David Craig, bandman in the 64th Regt of Foot and Bridget Gill, spinster of this Parish, were married in the Collegiate Church of St Nicholas, after banns duly published also William Simpson of said Regt and Letty Dolan, after banns likewise published, by me, H. Morgan, Vicr for Revd J. Whitley, G[arrison] C[haplain]

[Page] 79

Decr 27th 1828, baptized William Thomas son of John Burke of Moyglas in the County of Galway and of Emily his wife, born Decr 19 1828, H. Morgan, Vicr

December 29th 1828, baptized Lyddy daughter of John Waterson, Private Soldier in His Majesty's 64 Regiment of Foot and of Margarette his wife, born Decr 21st 1828, H. Morgan, Vicr

December 31 1828, baptized Jane daughter of John Kenny, nailer and of Jane his wife, born October 24 1828, H. Morgan, Vicr

Jany 25 1829, baptized Mary daughter of Norman Ashe, Collector of Excise and of Margarette his wife, born Jany 16 1829, H. Morgan, Vicr

Jany 31 1829, baptized Charles Ruxton son of Dennis Potter, attorney and of Isabella his wife, born Jany 21 1829, H. Morgan, Vicr

Feby 1st 1829, baptized George son of John Wheeler, ropemaker and of Margarette his wife, born Jany 18 1829, H. Morgan, Vicr

Feby 11 1829, James Richardson of Roscrea and Catharine Maxwell, of this Parish, were married by licence from the Archbishop of Tuam, by me, H. Morgan, Vicr

[Page] 80

March 2 1829, baptized Priscilla Mary daughter of Thomas Smith, mariner of Milford, South Wales and of Jane his wife, born Feb 24 1829, H. Morgan, Vicr

Baptized March 16 1829, Frederick Richard son of John & Catharine Prosser, 64th Regt, J. Whitley, G[arrison] C[haplain]

March 17th 1829, James Duncan of the city of Dublin & Susanna Irwin, spinster of this Parish, were married by license, in the Collegiate Church of St Nicholas, by me, James Daly, Warden
Witness present Harloe Irwin, Harloe Dennis

May 30 1829, baptized James son of William Giles, navy pensioner and of Mary his wife, born May 26, H. Morgan, Vicr

[Page] 81

Baptized March 22nd 1829, Anne Jane daughter of Patrick and Catharine Pipper, 64th Regt, J. Whitley, G[arrison] C[haplain]

April 12 1829, baptized Caroline Belinda daughter of Valentine Browne and Frances his wife, born March 31 1829, H. Morgan, Vicar
May 24 1829, baptized John Maxwell
May 31 1829, baptized Eliza daughter of James Chambers, haberdasher and Ellen his wife, born May 27 1829, H. Morgan, Vicr
June 14 1829, baptized David son of Sergeant John Brooke, 75th Regt and of Bethy his wife, born June 13 1829 and James son of Private James Robertson, 75th Regt and of Margarette his wife, born June 12 1829, H. Morgan, Vicr for Revd John Whitley, G[arrison] C[haplain]
June 14 1829, baptized William Charles Rowan Cashel son of Henry Cashel and of Arabella his wife, born June 4th 1829, H. Morgan, Vicr

[Page] 82

August 10 1829, baptized Richard son of John Brew of Kilrush in the County of Clare and of Eliza his wife, born August 7 1829, H. Morgan, Vicr
August 16 1829, baptized Anne daughter of Richard Swan and Catharine his wife, born Aug. 10 1829, H. Morgan, Vicr
Septr 6th 1829, baptized William son of George McLachlan, Private Soldier in His Majesty's 75th Regt of Foot and of Margarette his [blank], born Septr 4th 1829, H. Morgan, Vicr for the Rev John Whitley, Garrrison Chaplain
October the 5th 1829, Nicholas Edward Browne Esq. of Woodstock & Mary Browne, spinster of Galway, were married by license from the Court of Tuam, in the Collegiate Church of St Nicholas at canonical hours, by me, James Daly, Warden of Galway
Witness present Michl Browne, Danl Foley, Jno. Steadman

[Page] 83

October 11 1829, Charles Henry Le Poer Trench Morgan, son of the Rev Henry Morgan and of Ellen his wife, born October 7th 1829, was baptized, by me, H. Morgan, Vicar
October 24 1829, baptized Melvin, son of Melvin McGregor, Private Soldier in his Majesty's 5th Regt of Foot and of Sarah his wife, born October 17 1829, H. Morgan, Vicar

November the 7th 1829, Munty Glynn & Honor MacMahon were married by license from Tuam, in the Collegiate Church of St Nicholas, by me, James Daly

Novr 9th 1829, David Glennan and Anne Murphy, spinster, were married by license from Tuam, in the Collegiate Church of St Nicholas, by me, H. Morgan, Vicr

Novr 10th 1829, born Charles Augustus North son of Brownlow North Esqr and Grace Anne his wife, baptized Novr 19th by his grandfather, Thos Coffey

January 11th 1830, born Thomas Herbert son of the Revd Edward Eyre Maunsell and Eliza Maria his wife and baptized the 25th January by his father, Edw. Eyre Maunsell

[Page] 84

Nov. 10 1829, baptized Andrew son of Michael Costello of Tuam and of Mary his wife, born Novr 4th 1829, H. Morgan

Novr 12 1829, baptized Mary Ellen daughter of James Kearney Esqr, Comptroller of Customs and of Eliza his wife, born October 31 1829, H. Morgan, Vicr

Decr 13 1829, baptized Patrick son of Hugh Higgins, pensioner and of Ruth his wife, born Decr 4th inst, H. Morgan, Vicr

Decr 27 1829, baptized James son of John Maxwell and of Catharine his wife, born Decr 20 1829, H. Morgan

Jany 6th 1830, Henry Smyth of the Arran Water Guard and Ellen McDonnell, spinster, were married by license from the Archbishop of Tuam, by me, H. Morgan, Vicr
Witness present John Steadman, Henry Caddy

[Page] 85

Jany 17th 1830, William Dobbin and Elizabeth Gallagher were married by license from Archbishop of Tuam, by me, Edwd Bourke, Vicar
Witness present Henry Caddy

Feby 7th, baptized Bridget daughter David Hynes and Winefrid his wife, H. Morgan

Feby 8th 1830, baptized Mary Sarah daughter of John Burke of Moyglass and of Emily Sarah his wife, born Jany 17th 1830, H. Morgan, Vicar

Feby 12th 1830, baptized James Thomas son of Major Thomas Mahon of Bellvill in the County of Galway and of Jane his wife, born Feby 5 1830, H. Morgan, Vicr

Feby 24th 1830, baptized Martha daughter of James D. Dale, soldier in the 5th Foot and of Elizabeth his wife, born Feby 11 1830, H. Morgan, Vicar

March 2nd 1830, baptized Catharine daughter of William B. Stephens and Catharine his wife of Newcastle Distillery, born Septr 8th 1829, H. Morgan, Vicar

[Page] 86

March 7th 1830, baptized Joseph son of James O'Brien, clerk of the Mail Coach Office and of Margarette his wife, born March 2nd 1830, H. Morgan, Vicar

March 9th 1830, baptized William son of John Harrison of the Custom House, Waterford and of Jane his wife, born February 5th 1830, H. Morgan, Vicar

April 6 1830, baptized Ellen daughter of Henry and Martha Boyd of the Water Guard, born 1st of January 1830, Edw. Eyre Maunsell

April [blank] 1830, baptized John son of John and Margaret Dennisson of Lenaboy, gardener, born Easter Saturday 10th April 1830, Edw. Eyre Maunsell

May 26th 1830, Thomas Burke and Ellen Burk, spinster, both of Roxbro' in the County of Galway, were married by license from the Archbishop of Tuam, by me, H. Morgan, Vicr

[Page] 87

Baptized John Nicholas[46] Burdge, the 25th of April 1830, John D'Arcy
Baptized John Browne, on the 2nd of May 1830, John D'Arcy
May 4th 1830, baptized Robert son of Dennis Bowes Potter and of Isabella his wife, born April 24th 1830, H. Morgan, Vicr

---

[46] The name John appears to be added in after Nicholas at a later date.

May 9th 1830, baptized Sarah daughter of Stephen Browne, Private Soldier in his Majesty's Fifth Regiment of Foot an[d] of Mary his wife, born April 20 1830, H. Morgan, Vicar for the Revd John Whitley D.D., Garrison Chaplain
James McDermot and Catherine Chevers were married by banns duly published, this 17th day of May 1830, by me, Edwd Bourke, Vicar
Henry Caddy
1830 June the 4th, baptized Caroline daughter of James Harris, Waterguard & Mary his wife, James Daly, Warden

[Page] 88

May 7th 1830, baptized Charles Gideon son of William Thomas (of the Waterguards) and Eliza Thomas, born 28th Apl 1830, Edwd Bourke, Vicar
Jany 3rd 1830, baptized John Davis son of George Davis of Waterguard and Anne Davis his wife, born 2nd of Jany, Edwd Bourke, Vicar
Jany 27th 1830, baptized Patrick son of Charles and Anne Smyth, born 22nd Jany, Edwd Bourke, Vicar
March 22nd 1830, baptized Charles son of John and Margt Wheeler, born 17th March, Edw. Bourke, Vicar
May 16 1830, baptized Frances Maria Hobard, John D'Arcy
July 18th, baptized Eliza Kelly, J. D'Arcy
July 25, baptized Mary Ann Chambers, John D'Arcy

[Page] 89

July 26 1830, Henry Slow, pensioner and Nancy Prendergast, spinster, were married after banns duly published, by me, H. Morgan, Vicr
July 27 1830, John Powel and Sarah Egan, spinster, were married by me, in the Collegiate Church of St Nicholas, by license from the Archbishop of Tuam, by me, H. Morgan, Vicar
Witness present: Jno. Steadman
Augt 1st 1830, Peter Gannon and Margarette Berry were married by license from the Archbishop of Tuam, by me, H. Morgan, Vicr
Augt 20, baptized Samuel son of Hugh Frazer of the County Down and of Eleanor his wife, born 13th ulto, H. Morgan, Vicar

September 9th 1830, baptized Louisa daughter to Mr Lambert of Castle Ellen, James Daly, Warden

Oct. 25th 1830, John Brown and Bridget McGowa[n] were married by banns duly published, in in the church of St Nicholas, by Edw. Bourke, Vicar
Present: Henry Caddy

[Page] 90

December the 11th 1830, Thomas Edward Blake Esq. of Menlo in the county of the town of Galway & Letitia Maria O'Brien, spinster of said town, were married in the Collegiate Church of St Nicholas, by license from Tuam and an order from the Court of Chancery according to the rites & ceremonies of the Church of England & Ireland by law established, by me, James Daly, Warden of Galway
Witness present Chas Bruway, Thomas O'Brien, Henry Caddy

Joseph Webb of the Waterguard and Agnes Day were married after banns duly published, this 10th day of May 1831, by me, Edw. Bourke
Witness present: Jno. Steadman

[Page] 91

Decr 9th 1830, baptized Frances daughter of Mr Rowland Stephens, watchmaker and of Susan his wife, born Decr 2 1830, H. Morgan, Vicar

Decr 9th 1830, baptized Rosanna Johnson daughter of James Kearney Esq., Comptroller of the Custom House, Galway and of Eliza his wife, born Novr 20th 1830, H. Morgan

February 9th 1831, married this day after the banns had been duly published, Thomas Flanagan and Rebecca Perry, both of this Parish, John D'Arcy

February 15th 1831, Thomas Maxwell & Mary Quigly were married in the Collegiate Church of St Nicholas, by license from Tuam, James Daly, Warden of Galway
Witness present John Quigley, Henry Caddy

[Page] 92

Feby 19th 1831, Wm Kerr, Sergt Major 28th Regt to Mary Ann Hamilton, by license from Abh. [Archbishop] of Tuam, J. Whitley, G[arrison] C[haplain]

Febr. 20th 1831, baptized James son of Thomas Walsh of the town of Roscommon and of Margarette his wife, born Jany 25th 1831, H. Morgan, Vicar

Baptized 25th September 1831, Georgiana Maria daughter of Alexander & Dorinda Ruxton, John Whitley, G[arrison] C[haplain], 25th Septr 1831

Baptized October 2nd 1831, Jane daughter of Sergeant William & Mary Hare, 28th Regt, John Whitley, G[arrison] C[haplain]

February 25 1831, baptized John Stratron, John D'Arcy

February 28th 1831, Samual Richardson, nailer, of this town and Eliza Maxwell, spinster, also of this town, were married in the Collegiate Church of St Nicholas, after banns duly published; by me, H. Morgan, Vicar

February 26th 1831, baptized Edward Macleery son of William & Hannah of the Prevention Service, James Daly, Warden

[Page] 93

February 26th 1831, baptized William Darne son of John & Honor of the prevention service, James Daly, Warden

Baptized George Thomas Glennan at his father's house, on the 11th of February 1831, John D'Arcy

April 26th 1831, John McNeice & Mary McLoughlin were married in the Collegiate Church of St Nicholas, by license from Tuam, James Daly, Warden

Witness present: Jno. Steadman, Henry Caddy

May 2nd 1831, James Filtus, policeman & Jane Balford, spinster, were married in this Collegiate Church, after banns duly published, by me, James Daly, Warden

Witness present: Jno. C. Ffrench, Henry Caddy

[Page] 94

Willliam Murray and Harriet Scott were married by license from the Archbishop of Tuam, this 12th day of May 1831, Edw. Bourke, Vicar
Witness present John Steadman
John Moran and Mary Concannon were married in church, after banns duly published, this 27th day of June 1831, by me, Edw. Bourke, Vicar
Witness present: Jno. Steadman
James Gibbons and Catherine Cox were married in the church, by license from the Archbishop of Tuam, this 2nd July 1831, by me, Edw. Bourke, Vicar
Witness present: Jno. Steadman
Patk Leonard and Jane Gamble were married by license from the A[rch]bishop of Tuam, in church, this 4th Augt 1831, by me, Edw. Bourke, Vicar
Jno. Steadman

[Page] 95

Septr 1 1831, baptized Eliza daughter of John O'Brien and of Margarette his wife, born Aug 27 1831, H. Morgan
Septr 25 1831, baptized Samuel son of Charles Tounsille and of Anne his wife, born Septr 16 1831, H. Morgan, Vicar
Baptized January 24th 1832, William son of Wm and Rose Iggs, 68th Regt, John Whitley, G[arrison] C[haplain]
Decr 3 1831, baptized Charles son of Timothy Glynn and of Mary his wife, born Decr 1 1831, H. Morgan, Vicar
Jany 8 1832, baptized Sarah daughter of Hospital Sergeant Thomas Pope, 68th Light Infantry and of Elizabeth his wife, born Decr 10 1831, H. Morgan, Vicar
Jany 17 1832, baptized Jessy daughter of Charles Copeland, Manager of the Provincial Bank, Galway and of Euphemia his wife, born Jany 5 1832, H. Morgan, Vicar

[Page] 96

Feby 6 1832, William Porter, pensioner and Bridget Martin, spinster, were married by license from the Archbishop of Tuam, by me, H. Morgan, Vicar

February the 23 1832, John Reid of the town of Galway and Mary Adamson, spinster, were married by license, in the Collegiate Church of St Nicholas, by me, James Daly, Warden of Galway
Witness: Patrick Reed, Henry Caddy, Jno. Steadman, Joseph Caddy
May 21 1832, Abraham Royse of Oucterard and Janet Lynch of Galway, spinster, were married in the Parish Church of St Nicholas, by licence from the Archbishop of Tuam, by me, H. Morgan
Richard M. Lynch, Jno. Steadman

[Page] 97

May 31 1832, baptized Jane Caroline daughter of David Persse Esqr and of Sarah his wife, born April 26th 1832, H. Morgan, Vicar
Robert Telford and Anne Knight were married by license from the A[rch]bishop of Tuam, this 15th day of June 1832, Edw. Bourke, Vicar
Jno. Steadman, Joseph Caddy
October 14 1832, baptized Henry Jackso[n] son of William Henry Spelman of the Coastguard Service and of Amelia his wife, born September 10 1832, H. Morgan, Vicar
July 29 1832, baptized Jane Matilda daughter Sergeant Deacon, 34th Regt and of Jane his wife, born the 24th inst, H. Morgan, Vicar
September 15 1832, baptized Margarette Johnson daughter of James Kearney, Comptroller of Customs and of Eliza his wife, born the 28th of August 1832, H. Morgan, Vicar
October 20th 1832, baptized Richard son of John O'Brien and of Margarette his wife, born the 16th inst, H. Morgan, Vicar
Jany 11 1833, baptized Elizabeth Jane daughter of William McCleery of the Prevention Service & Hannah his wife, John D'Arcy

[Page] 98

August 3 1833, baptized Lucia Adelaide daughter of Henry Cashell Esq. and of Arabella his wife, born July 26 1833, H. Morgan, Vicar
July [blank] 1833, baptized William son of John and Anne Ffrench, James Anderson
Septr 10 1833, James Valentine Browne of Arrandale and Mary Jane Blake of Brownville, were married in the Parish Church of St Nicholas, by license from the Archbishop of Tuam, by me, H. Morgan, Vicar

Witness present: Anth. J. Blake, Edmond Browne, Joseph Blake
Henry Caddy, Sexton   Henry Manning, Clarke
Septr 26 1833, Peter John O'Flaherty of Galway and Winefred Emily Flanigan of Galway, were married in the Collegiate and Parochial Church of St Nicholas, after banns duly published, by me, H. Morgan, Vicar
Present: Robert Mc Solde   Henry Caddy, Sex[t]on

[Page] 99

September 14 1834, baptized Eleanor Sarah Johnston daughter of James Kearney, Comptroller of Customs and of Elizabeth his wife, born September 4 1834, H. Morgan, Vicar
March 2 1834, baptized Elizabeth daughter of Thomas Slater, Private Soldier in his Majesty's 30th Regt of Foot and of Catharine his wife, born Feby 22 1834, H. Morgan

[The small number of entries on this page reflects the coming to the end of entries, the next page reverts to 1812]

[Page] 100

This is to certify that J. J. Bricknell Esq. of the Parish of Loughrea and Maria Blake Kenny, spinster, of the town of Galway, were married in the Parish Church of St Nicholas at the hour of eight in the morning, on the eleventh of September 1812, by me, James Daly, Warden
In the presence of Henry Cox, Henry Caddy
Michael Mahon & Maria Howard were married in this Church according to law, February 14th 1818, James Daly
Witness Dr Stanley, Jno. Steadman
Thos Shildrick & Mary Fitzpatrick married, March 18 1818, in this Church, by me, James Daly
Baptized John Swan, April 24 1818, Jas Daly
John Sullivan & Deborah Simpson were married by me, in the church of St Nicholas, April 25th 1818, James Daly
William Wheeler, Jno. Steadman

[Page] 101

[P?]at McDermot[47]
William Brandish & Margaret T[ooring] were married by me, June 23 1818, James Daly
Witness Jno. Steadman
Thomas [Now]lan & Mary Whelan married by publication, in the church of Mt Shannon, certified by Revd Mr J. Martin, Vicar and approved by Mr Daly, J. Whitley, G[arriso]n Chaplain, May 15th 1819
Jno. Steadman
James Barnet & Sarah Schahill married by publication, in the church of Athenry, as certified by the Revd Mr Irvine, Curate of Athenry, J. Whitley, G[arriso]n Chaplain, July 7th 1819
Joseph Bayley and Jane Campbell were married by me, September the 6th 1819, Danl Foley for J. Whitley, G[arriso]n Chaplain
Jno. Steadman
R[ichar]d Tarleton & Elinor Moran by publication, March 28th 1820, J. Whitley

[Page] 102

January 26th 1823, baptized Catharine daughter of Thos and Catharine Oakes, 3rd Vetn Battalion, J. Whitley, G[arrison] C[haplain]
November 29th 1823, baptized Biddy Mannion, James Daly
November 13th 1823, baptized Matilda Charlotte Lawrence daughter of Mr Lawrence of Belleview, James Daly
November 21st 1823, baptized William Wilson son to Mr Wilson of High St, James Daly
November 24th 1823, married by banns this morning at 10 o'clock, Patrick Ryan to Eleanour McDonough, both of this Parish, John D'Arcy
November 27th 1823, baptized Matthew Coughlan of Rahoon Parish, James Daly
Decr 27th 1823 [blank]

---

[47] This may be the beginning of an incorrect entry for the marriage of Patrick Furlong and Anne McDermot which took place on the 18 June 1818, see the marriage entry on page 110 of the register.

May 13th 1824, baptized at Oranmore, John son of Henry and Anne Minchin of the Police, James Daly

December 26th 1825, baptized at Oranmore, George Woods son of Benjamin and Anne, James Daly

[Page] 103

Baptized Mary daughter of John & Anne O'Neil, 3rd Vet. Battn, J. Whitley [no date]

George Gilchrist son of John Gilchrist and Catharine his wife baptized June 25th 1825, [the] said John [a] Private in the 1st Royal Vetn Batn, Thos Coffey

Ruth daughter of Nicholas Fitzsimons, Private Soldier of the 1st Royal Vetn Batn, July 7th 1825, Thos Coffey

Bridget daughter of Richd Bust, Private in the first Royal Vetn Batn, July 17th 1825, Thos Coffey

October the 12th 1825, baptized Jhon [sic] Francis son to Mr Cashel, Inspector of Fisheries, James Daly, Warden of Galway

December the 7th 1825, baptized Anne Ormsby Reilly daughter of John & Maria, James Daly

Baptized Alexander Dow, December the 18th 1825, James Daly

December 19 1825, baptized Maria Parker, James Daly

June 28 1826, baptized Robert & Catharine twins of Duncan & Elizabeth, both of Scotland, James Daly, Warden[48]

[Page] 104

Baptized June 18th 1826, John Forster son of John & Catharine Stone, 22nd Regt, J. Whitley, G[arrison] C[haplain]

August the 23rd 1826, Denis B. Potter Esq. & Isabella Ruxton, spinster, were married after license had from the Archbishop of Tuam, in the Collegiate Church of St Nicholas, by me, James Daly, Warden of Galway

Witness present: Michl Ormsby, Patt. Fynn, T. Ruxton

---

[48] This entry is repeated on page 113 where the surname is given as Campbell.

June 4th 1827, baptized William Henry Stoakes son to William Stoakes & Mary Anne his wife, James Daly, Warden of Galway

June 18 1829, baptized Marlow Miles Reilly[49] son to John Reilly of the Custom House & Maria his wife, James Daly, Warden

[Page] 105

Sept. 30th 1827, baptized Henry son of Henry Bright and Jane his wife, born Aug. 23rd 1827, H. Morgan

Feby 13 1828, baptized Maria Louisa daughter Thomas John O'Flaherty and Georgiana his wife, born Jany 11 1828, H. Morgan

June 4th 1830, baptized Antoniette Elizabeth daughter of William Kelly Wilton of Marino, County of Galway and of Mary his wife, born May 16th 1830, H. Morgan, Vicar

June 23 1833, baptized Margarette daughter of Henry Bright and of Jane his wife, born this day, H. Morgan, Vicar

January 22 1826, baptized Samuel Hamlet Littlefield son of Captain Kearney C. Littlefield and Susanna his wife, James Daly, Warden

[Page] 106

Octr 5th 1829, baptized Agnes & Margaret twin daughters of Rufus and Agnes Hollis, Sergeant 64th Regt, J. Whitley, G[arrison] C[haplain]

January the 17th 1829, John Walsh Esq. of Tuam & Eliza Mittchell, spinster of Galway, were married by license from Tuam, by me, James Daly

Witness present: [Walter] Mitchell, Pat. Fynn, David Mitchell

February 12 1832, baptized Charles Studdert Maunsell son of Edward & Eliza Maria of Fort Eyre, Shantalla, James Daly, Warden

September the 29th 1831, baptized Frances Anne daughter of John O'Hara & Lady Arabella O'Donnell his wife, James Daly, Warden of Galway

---

[49] The child's name is given as Miles Harloe Reilly in the index, Marlow appears to be correct see *BLGI* 1912.

[Page] 107

11th Oct. 1830, Peter Johnston and Bridgett Donahoe were married by banns duly published, in the church of St Nicholas, by me, Edw. Bourke Vicar
Witness present John Steadman, James Toole
March the 31st 1831, baptized Catharine Parker, John D'Arcy
April 2 1831, baptized Henrietta daughter of Richard Bloxham, Sargeant in the Police Establishment and of Honoria his wife, born 19th of February 1831, H. Morgan, Vicar
August 2 183[1], baptized Margarette daughter of Vivian Stephens of the Water Guard and of Mary his wife, born March 27 1831, H. Morgan, Vicar

[Page] 108

Decr 9 1828, baptized Thomas Christopher Shone son of Captain Kearney Cullen Littlefield of the ship *William* of Liverpool, merchantman and of Susan his wife, born Decr 7 1828, H. Morgan, Vicr
April 2 1830, baptized Eliza daughter George Brakley, Sergeant of the Constabulary Police of Tully Station and of Anne his wife, born Decr 17 1829 and
Eliza daughter of William Knight of same [Tully?] Police and of Lovedy his wife, born Decr 4 1829, H. Morgan, Vicar
Aug. 17th, baptized Euphernia Wilhelmina daughter of Charles Copland, Manager of the Provincial Bank in Galway and of Euphernia his wife, born August 9th 1830, H. Morgan, Vicr
August 29th 1830, baptized Mary Anne daughter of Thomas Smith, Private in His Majesty's 5th Regt of Foot and of Anne his wife, born July 26th 1830, for Revd John Whitley, G[arrison] C[haplain], H. Morgan, Vicr

[Page] 109

Decr 30 1828, baptized Anne daughter of of [sic] Dennis Bowes Potter and of Isabella his wife, born Decr 18 1828, H. Morgan, Vicr

Septr 5 1830, baptized Elizabeth daughter of Samuel Davidson, Corporal in His Majesty's 5th Regt of Foot and of Anne his wife, born August 28 1830, for Revd John Whitley, G[arrison] C[haplain], H. Morgan, Vicr

Novr 15 1830, baptized Benjamin Patrick Bloomfield son of Harlow Dennis and of Jane his wife, born Nov. 1 1830, H. Morgan, Vicar

October 23 1831, baptized Jane daughter of Dennis Divine and of Anne his wife, H. Morgan

Decr 9th 1831, baptized Matilda Jane, daughter of Robert Stephens, of Maderia Island Brewery and of Dorcas Diana his wife, born Novr 28 1831, H. Morgan, Vicar

[Page] 110

Patk Furlong & Anne McDermot were married in this Church, by licence from the A[rch]bishop of Tuam, by me, June 16 1818, James Daly
Witness Barney McDermot, Jno. Steadman

Francis Simpson & Honora Clancy married in this Church, by licence, July 7th 1818, by me, James Daly
Witness Edward Maxwell, Jno. Steadman

Patrick Moran & Frances Stewart married in this Church, by licence, July 25 1818, by me, James Daly
Witness C. Buclscenis, Jno. Steadman

Alexander Fraser to Catharine Munroe by licence, Septr 9th 1818, J. Whitley
Jno. Steadman

John Aiken to Mary Fayne by publication, Septr 22nd 1818, J. Whitley
Jno. Steadman

Thomas Forsayeth to Elenor Sullivan by leicence [sic] from the Archbishop of Tuam, March 3rd 1819, J. Whitley, G[arriso]n Chaplain
John Steadman

[Page] 111

Saml. Stephens & Sophia Killeny married in this Church, by license, 4th Oct 1818, by me, Edw. Burke
Witness James Killeny Jun., Jno. Steadman

I do hereby certify that Robert Wylie & Anne Blake were married by license from the Archbishop of Tuam, 23rd of January 1820, by me, James Daly

Witness Frans Blake, Jno. Steadman

December 10th 1822, married by banns John Hart & Mary Fahey, James Daly

December 3rd 1822, baptized John Greddington Benton

September 28th 1823, John Reilly & Maria Ormsby were married by license from the Archbishop of Tuam, in the Parish Church of St Nicholas, by me, James Daly

Witness present James Forster, Oliver Ormsby, John Reed, Jno. Steadman

[Page] 112

Baptized February 18 1824, Hugh son of Wm & Mary Quin, 1st Vetn Battn, J. Whitley G[arrison] C[haplain]

April 28th 1824, Mr William Blackburn of Gort and Miss Margaret Glyn of Galway, were married by license from Tuam, by me, James Daly, Warden of Galway

Witness present: Jno. Steadman, Patrick Glynn

May 1st 1824, Nicholas Burdge and Louisa McCartney were married by license from the Archbishop of Tuam, in this Church, by me, James Daly, Warden of Galway

Witness present Mary Tierney, James Forster

May 28th 1825, William Power Trench and Catharine Butler were married by license from the Archbishop of Tuam, in the Collegiate Church of Galway, by me, James Daly, Warden of Galway

Witness present: Geoffry Martyn, Edwd Eyre, Jno. Steadman

[Page] 113

Sept. 10th 1825, Benjamin Clayton and Margaret Donahue were married by license from the Archbishop of Tuam, in this Church, by me, Danl Foley

September the 28th 1825, John Loxton, mariner & Mary Hogan, spinster, were married after banns duly published, in the Collegiate Church of Galway, by me, James Daly, Warden
Witness present: Jno. Steadman
Married May 29th 1826, James Barnshaw of the 22nd Regt to Johanna Connel, by publication of banns, J. Whitley, G[arrison] C[haplain]
July 9th 1826, Elizabeth, daughter of Joseph Spright, Private Soldier in the 22nd Regt of Foot and of Johanna his wife, was baptized by me, in the Parish Church of St Nicholas, Galway, H. Morgan, Vicr for Rev. J. Whitley, Garrison Chaplain
May the 30th 1827, baptized James Bowden son to one of the Coast Guard, James Daly, Warden
June 28 1826, baptized Robert & Catharine twins of Duncan & Elizabeth Campbell, both of Scotland, James Daly, Warden

[Page] 114

Novr 18 1830, Edward Trott Wells of the Prevention Waterguard and Margarette Kilkelly, spinster, both of the Parish of Rahoon, were married by license from the Archbishop of Tuam, by me, H. Morgan, Vicar
Witness George Blake, Jno. Steadman
May 1st 1831, baptized John son of Joseph Holles, Private Soldier in his Majesty's 28th Regt of Foot and of Ellen his wife, born April 16 1831, H. Morgan, Vicar
Novr 6th 1831, baptized Dennis George son of Dennis Bowes Potter and of Isabella his wife, born Octr 17 1831, H. Morgan, Vicar

[Page] 115

Baptisms
Baptized Elizabeth Rebecca daughter of John Hockland, Drum Major of the 22 Foot and Leah his wife, this 19th day of April 1826, born Jan. 15th 1826, Thos Coffey
Baptized May 29th 1826, Christop[he]r son of John & [blank] of the 22nd Regt, J. Whitley

Baptized February 12th 1829, William Crofton son of William Cuthbert and Alexander Jessie Ward of the corps of Royal Engineers, J. Whitley, G[arrison] C[haplain]

I do certify that William Wallace and Anne Maria Melville were married by licence from the Archbishop of Tuam, 22nd day of Feby 1830, by me, Edw. Eyre Maunsell
Witness John Steadman, Thomas Malley

I do certify that John Huse and Biddy McDonal were married by banns, the 22 Feby 1830, by me, Edw. Eyre Maunsell
Witness John Steadman

14th March 1830, Jane Carr daughter John Carr of Waterguard and Jane his wife, baptized by me, this 14th March 1830, Edw. Burke, Vicar

[Page] 116

Novr 4th 1828, married John Joll, Private 64th Regt to Margaret Thompson, by publication of banns, J. Whitley, G[arrison] C[haplain]

March 30th 1829, Wm Briscoh, Private 64 Rgt to Catharine O'Brien, by publication of banns, J. Whitley, G[arrison] C[haplain]

September 25th 1831, baptized Alexander Chambers, John D'Arcy

October 12 1831, Gunning Plunketh Esq. of Cloone, Co Roscommon and Jane Kelly, spinster of Galway, were married in the Collegiate Church of St Nicholas, by license from Tuam, by me, H. Morgan, Vicar
Witness Jno. Steadman, Henry Caddy

Decr 28, baptized Jane daughter of Georg[e] Bently, 27 Decr 1831, H. Morgan

[Page] 117

Decr 28 1831, baptized William Henry son Henry Caddy, Sexton of the Parish of St Nicholas and of Mary his wife, born Decr 27 1831, H. Morgan, Vicar

Jany 29th 1832, baptized Jane daughter of John Knee, Private Soldier 5th Regt of Foot and of Mary his wife, born Decr 4 1831, H. Morgan, Vicar

February the 21st 1832, married John Pritchard, master of a vessel & Catharine Grehan of the town of Galway, by license from Tuam, in the Collegiate Church of St Nicholas, James Daly, Warden of Galway Witness James Grehan, Martin Grehan, Henry Caddy

Baptized Octr 2nd 1831, Jane daughter of Wm & Mary Hare, 28th Regt, John Whitley, G[arrison] C[haplain]

[Page] 118

March 4 1832, baptized John Thomas son of Thomas Browne, Sergeant in His Majesty's 34th Regt of Foot and of Mary his wife, born Feby 26 1832 and Catharine daughter of James Talmedge, Private in same Regt and of Anne his wife, born Feby 8 1832, H. Morgan, Vicar

March 5 1832, John Connell and Judy Caulfield were married after banns duly published, in the Parish Church of St Nicholas, by me, H. Morgan, Vicar

March 25 1832, baptized Richard Thomas son of James Barter of the Coast Guard and of Elizabeth his wife, born March 8 1832, H. Morgan, Vicar

March 17 1832, baptized James Wheeler, John D'Arcy

March 28 1832, baptized William son of James Killery and of Mary his wife, born March 22 1832, H. Morgan, Vicar

June 3 1832, baptized Isabella daughter of Joseph Harrison, Private Soldier in His Majesty's 34th Regt of Foot and of Matilda his wife, born May 26 1832, H. Morgan, Vicar

[Page] 119

Baptized Mary daughter of Charles and Nancy Smyth, this 3rd July 1832, born 15th June 1832, Edw. Bourke, Vicar

July 15 1832, baptized Sarah Ann Carr, John D'Arcy, Vicar

July 31 1832, baptized Eleanor McDonough, H. Morgan

June 17 1832, baptized William son of William Baird of the Revenue Police Establishment and of Catharine his wife, born June 13 1832, H. Morgan, Vicar

August 5 1832, baptized Edward son of William Grainger of the Police Establishment and of Mary his wife July 22 1832 and Frances daughter of Henry Buck and of Anne his wife, born July 19 1832, H. Morgan

Abraham Robt Marshall and Rachell Reid[50] were married in Church by license from the A[rch]bishop of Tuam, this 6th day of August 1832, by me, Edw. Bourke, Vicar

Present: Joseph Caddy, Henry Caddy

[Page] 120

Baptized Mary Anne daughter of Captain Ives and Elizabeth Stocker of the Royal Engineers, born June 8th 1832, Galway, July 9th 1832, John Whitley, G[arrison] C[haplain]

August 28 1832, Peter Donahoe and Margarette Conneely of Tully, were married after banns duly published, by me, H. Morgan, Vicar

Novr 18 1832, Richd Calcutt and Anne Fallon, spinster, were married in the Parish Church of St Nicholas by license from the Archbishop of Tuam, by me, H. Morgan, Vicar

Rob. R. Gray, Nicholas Colahan, Joseph Caddy

Greaves Redfern of the 67th Regt and Jane Eliza Hannon were married in Church, after banns duly published, this 27th day of Nov. 1832, Edwd Bourke, Vicar

Present Henry Caddy, Joseph Caddy, Thos Sweehins, Elizabeth Herbert

[Page] 121

Wm Benj. Hasler and Hannah Scott were married in Church, by license from the Archbishop of Tuam, this 19th day of Decr 1832, by me, Edwd Bourke, Vicar

Present Joseph Caddy, Henry Caddy

Jany the 13th 1833, baptized Alexander Burdge, John D'Arcy

[The following is written crossways on the page beside the above entry at a later date and in blue ink.]

---

[50] The words 'and Rachell Reid' were inserted after the original entry and are followed by the initials of H. Morgan and E. Bourke.

A. Burdge born Jan. 4, baptized Jan. 13, son of Mr Nicholas Burdge, jeweler & Louisa Macartey his wife, John D'Arcy, Vicar

February 25th 1833, baptized Jane Elizabeth MacCleary, John D'Arcy A.M.

March 27 1833, baptized William son of William Bastable Stephens of Newcastle and of Catharine his wife, born February 14 1833, H. Morgan, Vicar

April 28th 1833, baptized George son of Richard & Honoria Bloxham of the Police Establishment and Mary Jane daughter of Wm & Sophia Ware, 67th Regt, John Whitley, G[arrison] C[haplain]

[Page] 122

Married this morning by licence from the consistorial & metropolitical court of Tuam, Michael L. Travis & Margaret Berry, spinster, both of this Parish, John D'Arcy
Present Henry Manning, Clarke

Baptized Evelyn James son of Charles (Lieut in the 67th Regt) and Elizabeth James, dated this 31st day of May 1833, Edwd Bourke, Vicar [this entry is crossed out here but appears below on page 123]

Baptized William son of Vivien Stephens of the Water Guard and Mary his wife, the 2nd May 1833, born 27th Apl 1832, Edw. Bourke, Vicar

Baptized William son of Henry Boyd of the Water Guard and Martha his wife, born 17th May 1832, baptized 3rd June 1833 three, Edw. Bourke, Vicar

[Page] 123

John McNab and Teressa Regan were married in Church, by license from the Archbishop of Tuam, this 9th day of June 1833 three, Edw. Bourke, Vicar
Present: Henry Manning, Clarke

April 13 1833, baptized James son of Robert Threlford and of Anna his wife, born same day, H. Morgan, Vicar

April 15 1833, baptized Elizabeth daughter John George and of Mary his wife, born Apl 1 1833, H. Morgan, Vicar

James Evelyn son of Charles Woodcock James, Lieutenant in the 67th Regiment and Elizabeth Love his wife, was baptized in the Collegiate Church of St Nicholas in the town of Galway, this 31st day of May 1833, by the Revd Edward Burke Vicr, H. Morgan, Vicar

Anne daughter of John Dennison and Margaret his wife, was baptized in the Collegiate Church of St Nicholas in the town of Galway, this 7th day of July 1833, by me, Edw. Eyre Maunsell, Vicr

Fanny daughter of Hugh Brice White and Isabella his wife, was baptized by me, in the town of Galway, the 15th day of August 1833, Edw. Eyre Maunsell, Vicar

[Page] 124

July 30 1833, William Wynn and Ellen Grogan were married after banns duly published, in the Parish and Collegiate Church of St Nicholas, by me, H. Morgan, Vicar
Henry Caddy, Sexton

July 8 1833, Edward Grainger and Elizabeth Barry were married after banns duly published, in the Parish and Collegiate Church of St Nicholas, by me, H. Morgan, Vicar

August 5 1833, Henry Stuart and Mary Donahoe, spinster, were married after banns duly published, in the Parish and Royal Collegiate Church of St Nicholas, by me, H. Morgan, Vicar
Henry Manning, Clarke   Henry Caddy, Sexton

Joseph Bright and Mary Jane Patterson were married in church, by license from the Archbishop of Tuam, this 20th Octr 1833, by me, Edwd Bourke, Vicar
Henry Caddy, Sexton

[Page] 125

August 8 1833, Patrick Flynn and Maria Singleton, spinster, both of this Parish, were married by license from the Archbishop of Tuam, in the Parish and Collegiate Church of St Nicholas, by me, H. Morgan, Vicar
Witness present: James Singleton, Joseph Caddy

August 11 1833, Jonathan Salkeld and Mary Swan, spinster, were married by license from the Archbishop of Tuam, in the Collegiate Church of St Nicholas, by me, H. Morgan, Vicar
Henry Caddy, Sexton   Henry Manning
Baptized Monimia Morgan, born July 14 1833, H. Morgan
Married Octr 28th 1833, John Goddard, Sergeant of the 30th Regt of Foot to Hannah Yardley, by license, J. Whitley, G[arrison] C[haplain]
Henry Manning, Clarke   Henry Caddy, Sexton

[Page] 126

August 25 1833, baptized Thomas son of Sergeant John B[e]rry of His Majesty's 30th Regt of Foot and of Mary his wife, born August 1833, H. Morgan
August 25 1833, baptized Henry Edward son of Charles Fullick, drummer in his Majesty's 30th Regt of Foot and Eliza Ann his wife, born August 13 1833, H. Morgan
Baptized William Robert Efford son of John Efford of the 30th Reg., John D'Arcy, October 6th 1833 three
Octr 13 1833, baptized George Ruxton son of William Ruxton and Sabina Burke [a long line follows Miss Burke's name], born 24 Sept 1833, Edw. Eyre Maunsell[51]
October 20 1833, baptized Maria Susan daughter of William Abbott of the 30th Regt and Mary his wife, born the 6th instant, Edw. Eyre Maunsell
Octr 27 1833, baptized Jane daughter of Edward Quigley and Jane Quigley otherwise Booth, his wife, born 21 Octr inst, Edw. Eyre Maunsell
[blank] daughter of Edward Nethercoot and [blank], Edw. Eyre Maunsell, Octr 27 1833

[Page] 127

Baptized Stuart McConnell, John D'Arcy, Octob[e]r the 2nd 1833
Baptized Elinor Harriet daughter of Revd John & Ellen Whitley, January 23rd 1819, J. Whitley

---

[51] This child is recorded as illegitimate in the index.

Jane daughter of Revd John & Ellen Whitley, January 29th 1821, John Whitley

Mary daughter of Revd John & Ellen Whitley, October 25th 1822, John Whitley

John son of Revd John & Ellen Whitley, 1st February 1824, John Whitley

Emily Olivia Elizabeth[52] daughter of Revd John and Ellen Whitley, 27th February 1829, John Whitley

Charles James son of Revd John and Ellen Whitley, November 9th 1833, John Whitley

William Macnamara son of Richard and Ann Calcutt of Wellpark, August 8th 1833, John Whitley

Venon son of Venon and Frances Armstrong, Adjt of the 30th Regt, 6th November 1833, John Whitley

[Page] 128

Baptized Rose daughter of James & Bridget Graham, 64 Regt, 17th of Novr 1833, J. Whitley

Novr 21 1833, baptized Edward son of Thomas O'Brien of the Mail Coach Hotel and of Margarette his wife, born Novr 6th 1833, H. Morgan, Vicar

Jany 10 1834, baptized Cuthbert Fetherstone son of Lieutenant Robert Daly of his Majesty's 14th Regt of Foot and of Frances his wife, born Novr 19 1833, H. Morgan, Vicar

Jany 26 1834, baptized Harriet daughter of James Burgess of the 30th Regt of Foot and Mary Burgess otherwise Shaw, his wife, born 1 Jany 1834, Edw. Eyre Maunsell, Vicar

March 10th 1834, William Pratt, Private Soldier in his Majesty's 30th Regiment of Foot and Anne Hazlette, spinster, were married in the Parish and Collegiate Church of St Nicholas, after banns duly published, by me, H. Morgan, Vicar

Witness present Henry Caddy, Sexton

---

[52] The name Emily Louisa was originally entered, the Louisa was later crossed out and changed to Olivia Elizabeth by J. Whitley.

[Page] 129

Feby 9 1834, baptized Henrietta daughter of Joseph White, Private Soldier in His Majesty's 30th Regt of Foot and of Helen his wife, born Feby 4 1834, H. Morgan, Vicar

Feby 9th 1834, baptized John Michael son of Lieutenant John Hughes, half pay 82nd Regt and Margarette his wife, born 26th Jany 1834, H. Morgan, Vicar

Feby 9th 1834, baptized William Burdge son of Nicholas Burdge of High St, jeweller, John D'Arcy

Feby 16th 1834, baptized Jane daughter of Edwd Shea, Private in the 30th Regt, John D'Arcy

Feby 23 1834, baptized Thomas son of Thomas Chesterten, Private Soldier in His Majesty's 30th Regt of Foot and of Jane his wife, born Jany 31st 1834, H. Morgan, Vicar for Revd J. Whitley, G[arrison] C[haplain]

[Page] 130

March 16 1834, baptized James Donnell MacDonald son MacDonald of the 30 Regt, John D'Arcy

March 25 1834, baptized William James son of Edward Neville Dalton, Ch[ief] Off[icer] of the Coast Guard and Elizabeth Dalton, born 8 Nov 1833, Edw. Eyre Maunsell, Vicar

April the 6th 1834, baptized James White son of Harstery White of the 30 Regt, John D'Arcy

May 4th 1834, baptized Ann daughter of Wm and Catharine Taylor of the 30th Regt, John Whitley

May the 11 1834, baptized Maurice Ingle son of Maurice Ingle, Private in the 30th Regt, John D'Arcy

May 17 1834, Revd John D'Arcy, Vicar of St Nicholas and Isabella Rielly, daughter of John Lushington Rielly Esq. of Scarvagh House, County Down, Collector of Customs of the port of Galway, were married by license from the Archbishop of Tuam, by me, H. Morgan, Vicar

Henry Caddy, Sexton   Henry Manning, Clarke

[Page] 131

May 20 1834, George Rimminton, Sergeant in His Majestys 30th Regt of Foot and Isabella McDermott were married by license from the Archbishop of Tuam, in the Parochial and Collegiate Church of St Nicholas, by me, H. Morgan, Vicar
Witness present Joseph McDermott   Henry Caddy, Sexton   Harry Manning, Clarke
William Henry son of William Grainger of the Constabulary and Mary Grainger otherwise Berry[53], was baptized by me, this 15th day of June 1834, born 30th May 1834, Edw. Eyre Maunsell, Vicar
June 16 1834, baptized Jacob Benjamin Neugell Seaman son of Thomas Seaman, Private in his Majesty's 85th Regt of Foot and of Mary his wife, born June 1st, H. Morgan, Vicar
Emily Fitzsimons daughter of John and Anne Fitzsimons was baptized by the Revd E.Bourke, on the 3rd day of Feby 1833, H. Morgan, Vicar

[Page] 132

The sum of £15 given by Mrs Wilkins to the protestant poor of this Parish was dispersed of on Monday 24th of January 1820 as follows –

Banks, Mary	Neville, Peggy
Bently, John	Shaughnessy, J.
Blair, Mary	Smyth, Mrs
Blakely, John	Taggart, Mrs
Crudgeen, Mrs	Wild, Mrs
Carr, Anne	Swan, Mrs
Cox, John	Cullen, Mrs
Fairclough, Mrs	Anderson, John
Haliday, B.	Stuart, Mrs
Lacy, Bob	Glynn, Mrs
Lacy, Bob	Cusack, John
Mrs Macklin	Davis, Mrs
McDonough, Mrs	Sexton, Mrs
Norman, John	Sharp, Mrs
Norman, Stephen	Conolly, Mrs

---

[53] Berry appears to be Mary Grainger's maiden name in this entry, while Barry appears in her marrige entry on page 124 of the register.

Anthony Morris
Pue, John
Quigly, Mrs

Ramsay, Ab.

Murphy, B.
Williams, John
Anne Carr [there appear to be 2 entries]

5s to each	£9 5 ..
A.R.	5 .. ..
Divers	.. 2 6
Mullin, Mrs	.. 2 6
Ch. poor on Sunday	.. 10 ..

James Daly
Andw Rud   ) Church
James Forster)   Wardens

[Page] 133

1833 Novr, baptized Robert Grainger son of Robert Grainger, Edw. Eyre Maunsell
Decr 8, baptized Jane daughter of Thos Maxwell and Mary Quigley his wife, Edw. Eyre Maunsell
July 2nd 1834, baptized John Michael Ormsby[54], John D'Arcy
July 9th 1834, baptized John Darnell[55], John D'Arcy
July 13th 1834, baptized George son of Sergeant George Brookes of his Majesty [8]5th Regt and of Anne his wife, born June 22 1834, H. Morgan, Vicar
July 16 1834, baptized William son of Joseph Webb of the Coastguard and of Agnes his wife, born July 4th 1834, H. Morgan, Vicar
July 20th 1834, baptized Stephen son of Thomas Mac[kye], Sergeant Major of the Constabulary Police and of Margarette Deborah his wife, born July the 4th 1834, H. Morgan, Vicar

---

[54] Additional information in the index records that he was son of W. Ormsby of the Waterguards and Eliza his wife.
[55] Additional information in the index records that he was son of Darnel of the Waterguards, his parents were John and Honora, see other entries for children of this couple on pages 93 and 152 of the register.

July 19th 1834, baptized Margarette Sarah daughter of Mr John Reid and of Mary his wife, born July 10 1834, H. Morgan

[Page] 134

August the 15th 1834, Robert D. Persse Esq. & Mary Fanny Whistler of the town of Galway, were married by license from Tuam, at the Collegiate Church of St Nicholas, Galway, by me, James Daly
Witness present Thomas Moore Persse, Thomas Whistler, Parsons Persse, Henry Manning
September 3rd 1834, Anne daughter of Andrew Duncan, Private in the His Majesty's 85th Regt of Foot and Emma Duncan his wife, was this day baptized by me, in the Collegiate Church of St Nicholas. She was born 11 Augt 1834, Edw. Eyre Maunsell, Vicar
Sept. 6th 1834, baptized Robert John son of John Robert Fitzsimons, Gov[erno]r County Gaol and of Anne his wife, born August 26 1834, H. Morgan, Vicar
Sepr 6th 1834, baptized George son of Hugh Brice White and Sarah Isabella his wife, Edw. Eyre Maunsell, Vicar

[Page] 135

Septr 183[4], baptized Mary Anne daughter of Henry Little, pensioner from the 64th Regt of Foot and of Mary his wife, born Septr 7 1834, H. Morgan
October 25th 1834, Thomas MacMahon married to Mary Mullen by licence from Tuam, he is the armourer of 85th Regt, J. Whitley, G[arrison] C[haplain]
November 5 1834, baptized Elizabeth Allen daughter of [blank] Allen of the 85 Regt, John D'Arcy
Baptized Matthew Minehan son of Martin Minehan & his wife Catherine Salters of this Parish, John D'Arcy, Novemb[e]r 16 1834
Baptized Frederick Christopher O'Brien son of John O'Brien & Margaret his wife, John D'Arcy, Decemb[e]r 15 1834

[Page] 136

Baptized Mary Jane daughter of James Kerr, Private in the 85th Regt & Eliza his wife, John D'Arcy, 1834 Decr 21, December 21 1834 four [date is entered twice]
Baptized Richd Beard son of W. Beard & Catharine his wife, John D'Arcy, Decr 28 1834 1834 [this entry is crossed out, apart from D'Arcy's signature and the date]
Jany 21 1835, baptized Anna Maria daughter of John Hamilton, Revenue Officer and of Anne his wife, born Jan. 1st 1835, H. Morgan
Jany 22 1835, baptized Georgina Louisa Johnson daughter of James Kearney, Comptroller of the Custom House and of Elizabeth his wife, born Jany 14 1835, H. Morgan, Vicar
Jany 23 1834, baptized George Ward son of Philip Beere of the Coast Guard and of Jane his wife, born Jany 22nd 1835, H. Morgan, Vicar
1835 Jan. 25th, Mary Ann Gardiner, spinster, was interred in this Church yard, on this 25th day of Jany, aged as appears forty nine years – note the age marked on the coffin was fifty but this as alledged by her surviving friends is a mistake, John D'Arcy, Vicar

[Page] 137

John Browne & Mary Cassidy married after banns published, Feby 18 1817, by me, Jas Daly
James Henry Beatty and Charlotte Eliz[abe]th Jorible were married in this Church, on the 9th day of Apl 1833, by license from the Archbishop of Tuam, by me, Edw. Bourke, Vicar
Witness Henry Manning, Henry Caddy
William Martin, Private of the 85th Regt and Bridget Quin were married after banns duly published, this 29th day of Decr 1834, by me, Edw. Bourke, Vicar
Witness present [blank]
Baptized Isabella Jane Hill daughter of the Revd John Hill, Vicar of Donaghadee & Jane his wife, the 2nd day of January 1835 five, John D'Arcy
Baptized John Carr son of John Carr of the Coast Guard service & Jane his wife, the 3rd day of January 1835 five, John D'Arcy

[Page] 138

Jany 31 1835, William Butler Junr of Bunahow in the County of Clare and Ellen Lambert, spinster, of Castle Ellen in the County of Galway, were married by license from the Archbishop of Tuam, by me, H. Morgan, Vicar
Witness present Peter Lambert   Edward Lambert   Henry Caddy, Sexton   Henry Manning
Feby 8 1835, baptized Thomas Edward son of Joseph Caddy and of Margarette his wife, Feby 6 1835, H. Morgan, Vicar
March 8 1835, baptized William son of William Martin, Private Soldier in his Majesty's 85 L[igh]t Infantry and of Bridget his wife, born Feby 28 1835, H. Morgan, Vicar
March 17 1835, baptized Archibald son of Ambrose Rush of Dominick Street and of Anne his wife, born March 2 [18]35, H. Morgan, Vicar
Baptized Louisa daughter of Valentine Peter Hunter, L[ieu]t R[oyal] N[avy] & Chief Officer of the Coast Guards & Mary his wife, at Barna 17 March 1835, Edw. Eyre Maunsell, Vicar

[Page] 139

March 25 1835, baptized John son of John Davey, Corporal of the 85 Regt and Ellen his wife, born the 4th day of March 1835, Edw. Eyre Maunsell, Vicar
March 29 1835, baptized Caroline Sibella Morgan, born March 9 1835, H. Morgan, Vicar
April 12 1835, baptized Maria daughter of Thomas Davies, Private Soldier in His Majesty's 85 Regt and of Bridget his wife, born April 5 1835, H. Morgan
Baptized Sarah Jane daughter of Charles Duff of the 85th Regt Light Infantry and Margaret Duff otherwise Claxton, born the 6th Apl. 1835, April 19th 1835, Edw. Eyre Maunsell, Vicar
April 19th 1835, baptized Mary Anne daughter of James Richardson, nailor and of Catharine his wife, born April 15 1835, H. Morgan, Vicar

April 19, baptized Maryanne daughter of Valentine Peter Hunter, Chief of the Barna Coast Guard, H. Morgan, Vicar
Apl 19 1835, baptized George son of Robert Trelford of the Revenue Police and Anna his wife, born 16th April inst, Edw. Eyre Maunsell, Vicar

[Page] 140

John Ruane and Mary Anne Dalton were married in Church, after banns duly published, dated this 7th May 1835, by me, Edwd Bourke, Vicar
Present Henry Caddy, Sexton   Henry Manning, Clarke
June 8, baptized Benjamin son of John Wheeler and Margaret French his wife, born 15th May last, Edw. Eyre Maunsell, Vicar
James Sampson and Mary Anne Waters were married in Church, after banns duly published, this 8th day of July 1835, Edwd Bourke, Vicar
Henry Manning, Clarke   Henry Caddy, Sexton
July the 14 1834
[entry rubbed out] Baptized John [illegible] son of John [illegible] J. D'Arcy
July the 23rd, baptized Edward Johns son of [blank] Johns of the Coast Guard service & [blank] his wife, John D'Arcy [According to page 73 of the register the parents' names were George and Mary]
August 16, baptized Thomas son of Edward Quigley & Jane Booth his wife, born 11th Augt 1835, Edw. Eyre Maunsell, Vicar

[Page] 141

August 4th 1835, Alexander Donaldson of the West Paper Mills and Ellen Davis, spinster of Galway, were married by license from the Archbishop of Tuam, by me, H. Morgan, Vicar
Witness present: Martin O'Maly   Henry Caddy, Sexton   Henry Manning
Augt 17 1835, baptized Margarette daughter of Georg[e] Bentley, H. Morgan

Septr 1 1835, Willliam Handcock, boatman of the Coast Guard and Bridget Brown of this Parish, were married after banns duly published, in the Collegiate Church of St Nicholas, by me, H. Morgan, Vicar
Witness John Joe Murphy, Wm Neil, Henry Manning
Sepr 6, baptized Sarah Jane daughter of Samuel Parry, guard of the mail coach and Eliza Jane Harbeson his wife, child born Sepr 1st 1835, Edw. Eyre Maunsell, Vicar

[Page] 142

Septr 19th 1835, baptized Adelaide daughter of Peter Lambert Esqr of Castle Ellen in the County of Galway and of Mary his wife, born Septr 10, H. Morgan, Vicar
October 3rd 1835 baptized Robert Hamilton son of David McWalter, Private Soldier in His Majesty's 79th Regt of Foot and of Ellen his wife, born September 17 1835
October 24 1835 baptized Mary daughter of John Andrew Vining, Revenue Officer and of Eliza Steden his wife, born October 3 1835, H. Morgan
Novemb[e]r 8, baptized Ann Burdge, John D'Arcy
Decr 4th 1835, baptized John son of John & Rebecca Wright, born 14th Novr 1835, Edw. Bourke, Vicar
Decr 28 1835, Julian Cormick[56] of the Revenue Establishment and Mary Plunket, spinster of this Parish, were married by license from the Archbishop of Tuam, by me, H. Morgan, Vicar
Witness present Mich[ae]l Plunkett   Henry Caddy, Sexton   Henry Manning

[Page] 143

William Persse of Newcastle and Mary Anne Blake of Frenchfort, were married in Church, by license from the Archbishop of Tuam, on the 23rd day of Sepr 1835, by me, Edw. Bourke, Vicar
Present: Thos M.Persse   Charles Trounsell   Henry Manning
Henry Caddy, Sexton

---

[56] The name Plunket was originally entered then crossed out and Cormick written above and initialed twice by H. M[organ].

Richard Alexander Young of the Coast Guards and Susan Evans were married in Church after banns duly published, this 4th day of December 1835, Edw. Bourke, Vicar
Present Henry Caddy, Sexton   Henry Manning
Jany 20th 1836, Patrick Curtin, pensioner and Mary Morris, spinster, were married after banns duly published, in the Collegiate Church of St Nicholas, by me, H. Morgan
Jany 27th 1836, baptized Jane daughter of Joseph Webb of the Coast Guard and of Agnes his wife, born Jan. 6, H. Morgan, Vicar
Jany 17 1836, baptized Hope Hadden daughter of Lieut McEntire of the 78 Highlander Infy, born on the 25 Novembr 1835, John D'Arcy

[Page] 144

Feb 8 1836, baptized Anne daughter of William Bastable Stephens of Newcastle Distillery and Catharine his wife, six months old, H. Morgan, Vicar
Feby 17 1836, baptized Andrew son of Andrew Fife of Constabulary Police stationed now at Oucterard and of Bridget Welby, born Feby 4, H. Morgan, Vicar
March 14 1836, baptized Richard Tuthill son of Charles Trounsell of the Newcastle Distillery and of Anne his wife, born Jany 25 1836, H. Morgan, Vicar
March 20 1836 baptized Eleanor daughter of Henry Bright and of Jane his wife, H. Morgan, Vicar
April 12 1836, Thomas Lydon and Catharine Hair, spinster, both of this union, were married after banns duly published, by me, H. Morgan, Vicar
April 28 1836, baptized Anne daughter of Matthew Thomas Smith of Dangan Cottage and of Mary his wife, born April 23 1836, H. Morgan, Vicar

[Page] 145

April the 21st 1836, Mr David Henry and Miss Rachel Greham, both of Galway, were married by license from the Archbishop of Tuam, in

the Collegiate Church of St Nicholas, by me, James Daly, Warden
Witness present Anne Greham   Henry Caddy, Sexton
Baptized Charles Smith son of C. Smith & Mary Keating, John D'Arcy, May the 1st 1836
Baptized John Connel son of J. Connel & Catharine Dodgeworth, John D'Arcy, May 1 1836
Maria daughter of of John Dennisson & Margaret his wife was baptized in the Collegiate Church of St Nicholas, this 15 day of May 1836, born 21 Apr. 1836, Edw. Eyre Maunsell, Vicar
May 23rd 1836, Mr Redmond Burke and Miss Rose Browne, both of Galway, were married by license from the Archbishop of Tuam, in the Collegiate Church of St Nicholas, by me, Danl Foley
Henry Caddy, Sexton

[Page] 146

1836 May 26th, baptized Richard Martin son of John Martin (a carpenter), Edw. Eyre Maunsell, Vicar
June 5 1836, baptized Eleanor daughter of Patrick Ryan and of Ellen his wife, born April 27 1836, H. Morgan, Vicar
June 16th 1836, Robert Adams Esqr and Mary Susan Fry, both of this Parish, were married by license this day, [John] Armstrong, Vicar of Kiltoom. This marriage was duly celebrated between us Robert Adams, Mary Fry   Present J. [illegible], Oliver Fry
Baptized January 26th 1836, William son of Henry and Ann Briscoe, Captn R[oyal] E[ngineers], John Whitley

[Page] 147

Isabella daughter of John Connell (deceased) and [blank] his wife[57] was baptized by me, the 19th June and was born the 16 inst, Edw. Eyre Maunsell, Vicar
June 30 1836, William Downes Griffith Esqr and Elizabeth Arabella Poppleton were married pursuant to license by me, at the church of Kilcummen Oughterard, Edward Eyre Maunsell, Vicar

---

[57] John Connell, a shoemaker, died the day before his daughter was born. His wife was Judy Caulfield whom he married on 5 March 1832, see pages 118 and 439 in the register.

Saint John son of James Killery Esqr and Mary his wife was baptized by me, the 4th day of July 1836, born the 24 June 1836, Edw. Eyre Maunsell, Vicar

Married August 8th 1836, John Scot to Mary Caulfield by banns published, in this Church, John Whitley

Mary daughter of John Kelly and Mary Kelly otherwise Roland, his wife, was baptized by me, on the 11th day of August 1836, she was born the 3rd inst, Edw. Eyre Maunsell, Vicar

Septr 9th 1836, Octavius Chisolm Esqr and Malvina Lodge were married by me, pursuant to licence from the Archbishop of Tuam, in the Collegiate Church of Saint Nicholas, Edw. Eyre Maunsell, Vicar
Present Fran[ci]s Lodge, Henry Caddy, Henry Manning

[Page] 148

Henry Rea and Mary Doyle were married in church, by license from the Archbishop of Tuam, this 29th day of Augt 1836, by me, Edw. Bourke Vicar
Present Henry Caddy, Henry Manning

Emma daughter of William Gramsden of the Revenue cutter *Dolphin* and Susan Gramsden otherwise Pottle, his wife, was baptized by me, the 1st Sepr 1836, born 8th August, Edw. Eyre Maunsell, Vicar

Septr 4 1836, baptized Mary daughter of John Biggs, soldier of the 15th Regt of Foot and of Isabella his wife, born August 8 1836, H. Morgan, Vicar

September 4 1836, I baptized Lloyd Laing son of William Laing & Maria his wife, James Daly, Warden

Baptized Jane Richardson, John D'Arcy Vicar, Octr 26 1836, born 16th Oct.

[Page] 149

Baptized Mary Harding daughter of William J. Mulvany and Alicia his wife, this 15th day of Sepr 1836, who was born 29th July 1836, Edw. Bourke, Vicar

Septr 18 1836, baptized Edward son of Edward Grainger of Galway and of Elizabeth his wife, born on Septr 10 1836, H. Morgan, Vicar

Thos McGrath and Catherine Collins were married in church, by license from the A[rch]bishop of Tuam, this 25th day of Octr 1836, by me, Edw. Bourke, Vicar

October 28 1836, baptized William son of Richard Painter of the 15th Regt of Foot and Jane Painter otherwise Davis, his wife, born the 17th Octr inst, Edw. Eyre Maunsell, Vicar

Willm Granger and Mary Sockel, widow, were married in Church, after banns duly published, this 31st day of Octr 1836, by me, Edw. Bourke, Vicar

Walter McNally of the Police Establishment and Mary Taffy, daughter of one of the same establishment, were married by license from the Archbishop of Tuam, this 4th day of Novr 1836, Edw. Bourke, Vicar

[Page] 150

N[ovember] 3 1836, baptized Herbert son of James Blake Esqr of Invern Lodge and of Helen his wife, born Octr 16 1836, H. Morgan, Vicar

Married this day by licence from the Metropolitical Court of Tuam, Andrew Burk and Susan Thomas, both of this Parish, John D'Arcy, November the 30th 1836

Henry Caddy, Sexton   Henry Manning

Married this day by licence from the A[rch]b[isho]p of Tuam, Richard McDermott Esqr of Dublin and Elizabeth Lambert, daughter of Walter Lambert Esqr dec[ease]d of Castle Ellen, Edw. Eyre Maunsell, Vicar, December 3rd 1836

Richard McDermott   Eliz[abe]th Lambert   Henry Manning
Henry Caddy, Sexton

Baptized Georgina Mary daughter of James Stephens and Julia Mary Stephens otherwise Ingram, his wife, born and baptized December the 4th 1836, Edw. Eyre Maunsell, Vicar

[Page] 151

Decr 11 1836, baptized William son of John McMahon, Private Soldier in His Majesty's 18th Regt of Foot and of Catharine his wife, born Novr 27 1836, H. Morgan, Vicar

Decr 14 1836, baptized Mary daughter of Joseph Mason, Private Soldier in His Majesty's 15th Regt of Foot and of Anne his wife, born Decr 5 1836, H. Morgan, Vicar

Baptized John Edward son of James & Catharine Kenny, Galway, Decem[be]r 30th 1836, J. Whitley, G[arrison] C[haplain]

Margaretta Lucy daughter of Captain & Elizabeth Myers, 22nd Regt of Foot, Galway, Octr 30th 1836, John Whitley, G[arrison] C[haplain]

Mary Anne daughter of James Foran, shoemaker of Gort, Co Galway & Jane Kelly otherwise Foran, his wife, was baptized 1 Jany 1837, born 21 Decr 1836, Edw. Eyre Maunsell, Vicar

Anne Maria daughter of Robert Dudley Persse Esqr and Mary Persse otherwise Whistler, was baptized by me, this 19th day of Jany 1837, born 8 Jany 1837, Edw. Eyre Maunsell, Vicar

Baptized Rose infant daughter of Robert Tellford of the Revenue Police & Ann Wright his wife, this 26 day of January 1837, John D'Arcy A.M., Vicar of St Nicholas

[Page] 152

1837 Jany 29 Elizabeth daughter of William Chirm of the 15th Regt of Foot and Sarah Chirm otherwise Foster, his wife, was baptized by me, this day, she was born 25th Jany inst, Edw. Eyre Maunsell, Vicar

1837 Feby 5, Joseph son of William Williamson of the 15 Regt of Foot and Jane Williamson otherwise Nesbett, his wife, was baptized by me, this day, he was born 24 day of Jany 1837 seven, Edw. Eyre Maunsell

Feby 26 1837, baptized Henry son of John and Honora Darnel of the Barna Coast Guard Station, born Jany 31st, H. Morgan

Feby 26 1837, baptized Jane daughter of John and Margarette O'Brien of the Mail Coach Hotel, born Feby 21 1837, H. Morgan

March 12 183[7], baptized Letitia daughter of Frederick Elliott of the 15th Regt of Foot and Mary Elliott otherwise Goodwin, his wife, born Feby 26th 1837, Edw. Eyre Maunsell, Vicar

March 19, baptized Margarette daughter of Robert Bayly, drummer in His Majesty's 15th Regt of Foot and of Sarah his wife, born the 13 inst, H. Morgan

March 26 Easter Day, baptized Elizabeth daughter of Thomas Slow and Mary Anne Slow otherwise Reilly, his wife, born 24 Feby 1837, Edw. Eyre Maunsell, Vicar

March 27 1837, born Feby 3rd 1837, baptized Charles Vesey second son of John and Isabella D'Arcy at Vicarscroft in the Parish of Rahoon, John D'Arcy, Vicar, March 27 1837

[**Pages 153-154** were, at some point, cut out of the register. However, the index contains reference to 2 entries for page 153, the baptism of Archibold Rush and Susana Stephens, both of whom appear again on page 155].

[Page] 155

Baptized James son of James and Catherine Richardson, this 21st April 1837, child born 17th inst, Edw. Bourke, Vicar

Baptized Archibold son of Ambrose Rush Esqr and Anne Collis otherwise Rush, his wife, this 4th day of May 1837, born 16 day of April last, Edw. Eyre Maunsell, Vicar

May 7 1837, baptized Susan daughter of Rowland Stephens and Susan his wife, born April 8 1837, H. Morgan, Vicar

May the 14 1837, baptized John Stewart son of Alexander Stewart & his wife Bridget Stewart alias Connor, John D'Arcy A.M., Vicar

May 28 1837, baptized Armiah daughter of Sergeant William McLean of His Majesty's 15th Regt of Foot and of Eliza his wife, born May 12 1837 and Anne daughter of Richard Jordan, sailor and of Bridget his wife, born May 1st 1837, H. Morgan, Vicar

[Page] 156

1837 June 18, baptized William Henry son of William Renfry of the Coast Guards and Elizabeth Hoskins otherwise Renfry, his wife, born 6th June inst, Edw. Eyre Maunsell, Vicar

1837 June 18th, baptized Sarah daughter of William Deacers and Maria [blank] otherwise Deacers, his wife, born 11th June 1837, Edw. Eyre Maunsell, Vicar

June 25 1837, baptized Edward son of Edward Lyons of the 18th Royal Irish Regiment of Foot and of Anne his wife, born June 12 1837, H. Morgan, Vicar

Septr 6th 1837, married Gideon Delmage, Assist[an]t Surgeon 18th Foot to Julia Browne daughter of Mark Browne of Rockville Esqr, John Whitley, G[arrison] C[haplain]

Henry Manning, Clerk   Henry Caddy, Sexton

October the 12th 1837, baptized Andrew son of Mr Jno. Reid & Mary his wife, James Daly, Warden, born 26th Sepr 1837

[Page] 157

1837 Octob[e]r the third, baptized Honoria Greuber, born on the 26 of September, John D'Arcy

1837 Octr 18th, baptized Mary daughter of Thomas McGrath and Catherine McGrath otherwise Collins, his wife, born 29th Sepr 1837, Edw. Eyre Maunsell, Vicar

1837 Octr 25, I certify that Julian Anne daughter of Roderick O'Connor and Marianne O'Connor otherwise Morris, his wife, was received into the church, she having been baptized by me, at Rahoon, in the Parish of Rahoon, on the 14th day of August 1837, Edward Eyre Maunsell, Vicar of St Nicholas

1837 Octr 26, baptized Frederick Robert Cameron son of Malby Crofton Esqr and Sarah Jane Crofton otherwise Parke, his wife, born 13th Septr 1837, baptized at Arran View, Fair Hill, Galway, Edward Eyre Maunsell, Vicar

Jany 2 1838, Henry Manning, Parish Clerk of this Church and Charlotte Cotter, spinster of this town, were married by license from the Archbishop of Tuam, by me, H. Morgan, Vicar

Witness present George McNamara   Henry Caddy, Sexton

January 31 1838, baptized Clarissa daughter of Peter Lambert of Castle Ellen, James Daly, Warden

[Page] 158

1838 February 1st, married Patrick Cullen, Civil Assistant Royal Engineers to Mary Lambert, daughter of the late Patrick Sen. Lambert

of Oranmore[58] in the County of Galway, by license from the A[rch]b[isho]p of Tuam, Edw. Eyre Maunsell, Vicar
Patrick Cullen, Mary Lambert
Present Henry Caddy, Sexton   Henry Manning, Clerk
1838 February 10th, baptized Isabel Sabina daughter of John Land Wynn, Commander in Her Majesty's Navy and Elizabeth Lawrence Symons otherwise Wynn, his wife, born 7 June 1837, Edw. Eyre Maunsell, Vicar
1838 February 23rd, married George Gavin, Acting Constable of the Constabulary to Mary Benton, daughter of Henry Benton Locker of Her Majesty's Ware Houses at Galway, pursuant to licence from the A[rch]b[isho]p of Tuam, Edw. Eyre Maunsell, Vicar of St Nicholas
George Gavin, Mary Benton
Present H. Benton   Henry Caddy, Sexton   Henry Manning, Clerk

[Page] 159

Mathew Reed and Elen[o]r Wheeler, daughter of John Wheeler of Bohermore in the town of Galway, were married by license from the Archbishop of Tuam, this 26th day of Feby 1838, by me, Edw. Bourke, Vicar
Present: Jno. Reed   Henry Manning   Henry Caddy, Sexton
John Wilson and Anne McDonogh, daughter of the late Michael McDongh of Galway, were married by licence from the Archbishop of Tuam, this 26 day of February 1838, by me, Edw. Eyre Maunsell, Vicar
Present Henry Caddy, Henry Manning
Feby 25 1838, baptized Edwin Charles Thomas son of Charles Looker and of Jane his wife, born Jan 8 1838 and William Douro son of William Henry Spelman of the Barna Division of the Coast Guard and of Amelia his wife, born Feby 11 1838, H. Morgan

---

[58] Originally entered as 'the late Peter Lambert of Oranmore', 'Oranmore' then crossed out and 'Castle Ellen' entered. 'Peter' and 'Castle Ellen' crossed out and Patrick sen[ior] and Oranmore entered in a different pen and initialled E.E.M.

[Page] 160

Robt Monad, Private of the 8th Regt and Margt Coleman, spinster, were married in Church, after banns duly published, this 3rd day of March 1838, by me, Edw. Bourke, Vicar
Present Henry Manning, Clerk   Henry Caddy, Sexton
April 22 1838, James Douglass of the Revenue Police and Margarette Healy of Galway, were married by license from the Archbishop of Tuam, by me, H. Morgan, Vicar
Witness present Henry Manning, Clerk
September 8 1838, baptized Catharine Isabella daughter of Robert Persse Esqr of the Post Office & Mary his wife, James Daly

[Page] 161

Miles Kirwan and Maria Kirwin, spinster, were married by license from the A[rch]bishop of Tuam, the 22nd day of March 1838, by me, Edw. Bourke, Vicar
Present Henry Caddy, John A. Kirwan, Roderick J. Kealy
Joseph Webb son of Joseph Webb of the Coast Guard and of Agnes his wife was baptized by the Revd John Whitley D.D., on the 20th of May 1838, born April 27 1838, H. Morgan, Vicar
Amos Palmer Doolan of Derry House in the Kings Co. & Jane Barbara Smith, spinster, both residing at present in the Parish of St Nicholas, were married this day, by me, John [illegible initial] Law, Perpetual Curate of Eglish, Dio[cese] Killaloe, dated this 2nd October 1838
Present Thos Doolan Jun   Ralph Smith   Henry Smith   Henry Manning, Clerk Henry Caddy, Sexton

[Page] 162

Novr 23 1838, baptized privately at the Quarry House, Merlin Park, Charles Martin son of M.K. Blake & Julie his wife, John D'Arcy, Vicar

Archibald Phirls[59] and Maria Caddy were married in the church of St Nicholas, by license from the Archbishop of Tuam, on the eleventh day of February 1839, by me, Henry Morgan, Vicr
Edward Caddy, Henry Manning, Henry Bright
February 11 1839, baptized Louisa Mary eldest daughter of John and Isabella D'Arcy, at Vicars Croft in the Parish of Rahoon, John D'Arcy Vicar

[Pages 163-169 blank]

[Page] 170

Baptized the son of J. J. Bricknell, November 1813, James Daly
Decembr 12 1836, baptized Valentine Blake son of Thomas Blake Esq. and Maria his wife privately at their residence in this Parish, John D'Arcy, Minister

[Page] 171

Married Andrew Johnston to Fanny Anderson, both of Galway, by licence from Tuam, June 11th 1835, John Whitley
Henry Manning, Clerk   Henry Caddy, Sexton
Married after banns duly published in church – Michael Mullen to Catherine Crane, both of Galway, dated this 6th day of July 1835, Edw. Eyre Maunsell, Vicar
Present: Henry Caddy, Sexton
James Valentine Browne Esqr and Maria Griffin were married by me, pursuant to license from the Archbishop of Tuam, in the Collegiate Church of St Nicholas, July 1st 1837, Edw. Eyre Maunsell, Vicar
Present James McDonogh   Henry Caddy, Sexton   Henry Manning
July the 10, baptized John Dunbar D'Arcy eldest son of John and Isabella D'Arcy privately at Vicars Croft in the Parish of Rahoon, John D'Arcy, July 10 1835 five

---

[59] Appears under M as McPhirls in the index.

[Page] 172

Samuel Cross of Ballycar in the County of Clare and Maria Clarke of the town of Galway, were married in Church, by license from the Archbishop of Tuam, this 3rd day of August 1837, by me, Edw. Bourke, Vicar
Present: Henry Caddy, Sexton   Henry Manning
Alexander Digby Campbell and Cathne Fry were married by license from the Archbishop of Tuam, this 21st day of November 1837, by me, Edw. Bourke, Vicar
Present: Henry Caddy, Sexton   Henry Manning   Robert Adams
Baptized Mary Jane daughter of Thomas Gunberton and Catharine his wife, Gunberton is a Private in the Royal Sappers & Miners, John D'Arcy, Novemb[er] 26 1837
Baptized Sarah daughter of William Casey, a drummer in the 8th Regt and Eliza his wife, John D'Arcy, Novemb[er] 26 1837

[Page] 173

Baptized James son of James Burns and Rebecca Burns otherwise Price, his wife, born 23 Octr, Edw. Eyre Maunsell, Vicar
Baptized George Barlow, son of John Barlow, Colour Sergeant in the 8th Regt & Rosanna his wife, this 10th day of Decr 1837, John D'Arcy A.M., Vicar, Dec 10 1837
Decr 27th 1837, Edward Bell of Sunderland in the County of Durham, attached to the ship *St Patrick* of this town and Bridgett Cockerall of this town, spinster, were married by license from the Archbishop of Tuam, in the Parochial and Collegiate Church of St Nicholas, Galway, by me, H. Morgan, Vicar
Present Henry Manning   Henry Caddy, Sexton
December 31 1837, baptized William James son of Willian Laing & Maria his wife, James Daly, Warden

[Page] 174

April 3 1838, Henry McNamara son of the Revd Henry Morgan, Vicar, St Nicholas, Galway, and of Helen his wife, born March 25 1838, was baptized by the Revd John Whitley D.D., H. Morgan

[An entry of two lines has been completely blanked out and is impossible to decipher]
May 8 1839, Persse Lambert, School Master of Erasmus Smith's English Free School and Bedilia Cody, spinster, of this town were married in the Parish and Collegiate Church of St Nicholas, by license from the Archbishop of Tuam, by me, H. Morgan, Vicr
Witness present Henry Manning   Edward Caddy   Henry Caddy, Sexton
March 12 1840, baptized Francis son of Timothy Hogan of Arran Island and Catharine his wife, James Daly, Warden

[Pages 175-186 blank]

[Page] 187

20th of November 1828, I baptized, at Menlo Castle in the Parish of Oranmore, Arabella daughter of Sir Hugh O'Donnell & Arabella his wife, there being no church in the Parish, James Daly, Warden of Galway

[Pages 188-209 blank]

[Page] 210

W. Spelman & C. Winnett married by me, in the Church of Galway, after banns published, June 15 1812, James Daly, Minister
January 22 1820[6][60], baptized Samuel U. H. Littlefield son of Captain Kearny Littlefield & Susanna his wife, James Daly, Warden

[Pages 211–286 blank]

---

[60] This is most likely a duplicate entry, 1820 should read 1826.   Samuel Hamlet Littlefield was baptized on 22 Jan 1826, see page 105 of the register.

[Page] 287

March 1822 The interest of Mr Kirwan's bequest[61] amounting to £10 .. .. for the first half year was this day distributed among thirty one poor inhabitants of this town,
James Daly, Warden　　John Reed, Church Warden
December 20th 1822 the second half year's interest of Mr Kirwan's bequest was this day distributed as above,
James Daly, Warden　　John Reed, Church Warden
Present James Forster July 30 1823

The third half year's interst of Mr Kirwan's charitable bequest now vested in the new Government 4 per cent stock was this day distributed as above,
James Daly, Warden　　John Reed, Church Warden　　James Forster

Rec[eive]d one year's % Interest up to 1st of April 1823 £31.5.10.	Paid	
	March 1822	£10. .. ..
	December 20th Do	10. .. ..
	July 30th 1823	9. 15. ..
	Power of attorney	10. 10
	Balance in hand	1. .. ..
		31. 5. 10

[Page 288 blank]

---

[61] See introduction page

[Page] 289

		s d		s d
1st	Thomas Blakeny	£0.5.5.	Mr Bredun	£0.6.6.
2	Henry Bankes	.. 4.4.	Mrs Glynn	.. 4.4.
3	Mary Blair	.. 4.4.	Robert Lacy	.. 7.7.
4	Mr Carr	.. 6.6.	Mrs McLinn	.. 2.9½
5	Mr Case	.. 3.3.	Mrs Quigley	.. 5.5.
6	George Ferguson	.. 4.4.	Mrs Symth	.. 5.5.
..	Jane Reily	.. 4.4.	John Williams	.. 6.6.
..	James Wilde	.. 5.5.	Stephen Norman	.. 5.5.
..	Widow Coghlan	.. 5.5.	Peggy Shaw	.. 7.7.
	Mr Bradly	.. 2.9½	James Glynn	.. 2.9½
	Mrs Pugh	.. 5.5.	Mrs McDannel	.. 2.9½
	Sibby Shaugnessy	.. 2.9½	Mrs Roberts	.. 2.9½
				£2.19.10.
	George Wilde	.. 2.9½		2.17.1½
		£2.17.1½		£5.16.11½
			to rent of house	4.5.0.
				£10.1.11½

Distributed the above sum for the ease of 26 poor persons being the half yearly interest of Kirwan's Charity, October 24 1825
James Daly, Warden   Matt. Tho. Smyth, John Reed, C.W.s [Churchwardens]

[Page] 290

May 3 1827 distributed to twenty four persons the sum of 5.11.6 being (together with 4.10 the rent of poor house) the interest of Kirwan's Charity now vested in the Galway Savings Bank,
James Daly, Warden of Galway   John Reed, Church Warden

Distributed on the 5th of December 1831 the moiety of Kirwan's Charity interest remaining after rent of poor house. To the following 5s each:

+ Thomas Blakeny 1
+ William Bradly 1
+ Mrs Buckly +
+ Mrs Cox +
+ James Glynn +
 + Widow Glynn +
+ Widow Freeman +
+ Mrs McDonough -
+ Mrs McCarroll + -
+ John Maxwell + -
+ Mrs Piew + -
+ Mary Ramsay +
+ Jane Reilly +

[Page] 291

+ Mrs Roberts +
+ David Smith 1
+ Mrs Smyth 1
+ Sibby Shaughnessy + -
+ Mrs Quigly +
+ John Williams +
+ George Wylde + -

James Daly, Warden

Decr 7 1832 distributed the sum of £4.10.0. being a moiety of the interest of the interest [sic] of the Kirwan Charity to the following persons and in the following proportions:

Mrs McCarrol	£0.6.0.
John Maxwell	0.5.0.
Mrs Pugh	0.6.0.
Mrs Shaughnesy	0.6.0.
George Wyld	0.6.0.
Mrs Buckley	0.4.6.
Mrs Cox	0.4.6.

James Glynn	0.4.6.
Widow Glynn	0.4.6.
Mrs Freeman	0.4.6.
Mrs Lackey	0.4.6.
Mrs Reilly	0.4.6.
Mrs Roberts	0.4.6.
Mrs Quigly	0.4.6.
John Williams	0.4.6.

[Page] 292

Thomas Blakeny	0.3.0.
William Bradley	0.3.0.
Mrs McDonough	0.3.0.
David Smyth	0.3.0.
Mrs Smyth	0.3.0.
	4.10.0.

[Pages 293-306 blank]

[Page] 307

[3 signatures]
Mary Gibbons
Anne Costello
[illegible]
[Pages 308-437 blank with the exception of two pencil drawings and the signatures of Prudence Caddy, Thomas Caddy and Henry Caddy on pages 402-403]

[Page] 438

Obituary of the Parish of St Nicholas [burials]

Novr 1 1832, interred David Mitchell, who died October 30 1832, H. Morgan, Vicar

Jany 29th, John Ffrench, shoemaker, was interred in the churchyard of St Nicholas, who died Jany 27th 1834, H. Morgan, Vicar

Jany 19 1836, Hugh Edwards only son of Robert Edwards Esqr aged sixteen, was interred in the churchyard of St Nicholas. He died the 16th of January 1836, H. Morgan, Vicar, Edw. Eyre Maunsell, Vicar

Mary Strogen, widow aged 88 years, relict of the late John Strogen of this town was interred this 18th of March 1836, having died at Kilcolgan on the 16th instant, whose remains I attended, H. Morgan, Vicar

William Mason Esqr, aged seventy years, was interred in the church yard of Saint Nicholas. He died on the 19th of April 1836 & was interred the 20th Apl 1836, Edw. Eyre Maunsell, Vicar

Peter Ward Esqr, aged sixty years, was interred in the church yard of Saint Nicholas, on the 3rd day of June 1836. He died on the 1st inst, Edw. Eyre Maunsell, Vicar, H. Morgan, Vicar

[Page] 439

Malachy Hensley, a pensioner aged about 70 years, was interred in the church yard of Saint Nicholas on the 5 day of June 1836. He died on the 3rd inst, Edw. Eyre Maunsell, Vicar

John Connell, a shoemaker aged 28 years, was interred in the church yard of Saint Nicholas, on the 17th day of June 1836. He died on the 15th inst, Edw. Eyre Maunsell, Vicar

Jas Glynn, aged 90 years, was interred in the church yard of St Nicholas, on the 19th day of June 1836. He died on the 17th, Edw. Bourke, Vicar

Eliza Forbes, wife of William Forbes, was interred in the church yard of Fort Hill, on the 4th day of July 1836. She died on the 3rd inst, Edw. Eyre Maunsell, Vicar

William son of Robert Jolly of Ballinasloe, aged 10 months, was interred in the church yard of St Nicholas, on the 4th day of August 1836. He died on the 3rd inst, Edw. Eyre Maunsell, Vicar

Isaac Robson Esqr, aged 36 years, was interred in the church yard of Saint Nicholas, on the 15th day of August 1836. He died on the 13th instant, Edw. Eyre Maunsell, Vicar, Edw. Bourke, Vicar

Margaret Wilde, wife of George Wilde, upwards of 80 years old, was interred in the burial ground at Fort Hill, on the 5th day of Sepr 1836. She died on the 4th inst, Edw. Eyre Maunsell, Vicar

Richard Armstrong Esqr, aged 76 years, was interred in the church yard of Saint Nicholas, on the 13th day of September 1836. He died the 11th instant, Edw. Eyre Maunsell, Vicar

[Page] 440

William Fields, 15 Regt of Foot, was interred this day in St Nicholas church yard (aged 40 years), by me, Decr 31 1836, Edw. Eyre Maunsell, Vicar

William Buttery, Sergeant in His Majesty's 15th Regt of Foot, was interred in the church yard of St Nicholas, Galway, this 6th day of January 1837, H. Morgan

Anne Hinks daughter of John Hinks of the 15th Regt and Charlotte Hinks otherwise Callow, his wife, aged 3 years and 7 months, was buried in the church yard of St Nicholas, the 17th day of Jany 1837, by me, Edw. Eyre Maunsell, Vicar

James Kearney son of J. Kearney Esqr, Controller of Customs, was interred in the church yard of St Nicholas, the 24 day of Feby 1837, aged 11 years, Edward Bourke, Vicar & E. E. Maunsell, Vicar, present

Mrs Isabella Copland, widow of the late Wm Copland of St Elizabeths, Jamaica, was interred in the church of St Nicholas, the 10th of March 1837, Edw. Bourke, Vicar

John Lydon (a pensioner) was interred in the church yard of St Nicholas, the 11th day of Apl 1837 & three of his children were also interred in the same grave, viz Abraham 7 years old, Clement 5 years, both buried the 24 of May 1837 and Ellen 2 years old, buried the 23rd of June 1837[62], Edw. Eyre Maunsell, Vicar of St Nicholas

Edward Murphy (brazier) was interred in the church yard of Saint Nicholas, the 20th day of April 1837, aged 80 years, Edw. Eyre Maunsell, Vicar of St Nicholas

---

[62] The information regarding the children was added sometime after the initial entry in a different hand. The signature of Maunsell relates to the entry of John Lydon.

[Page] 441

John White Esqr was interred in the church yard of Saint Nicholas, the 5th day of August 1837, aged 65 years, Edward Bourke, Vicar officiated, Edw. Eyre Maunsell, Vicar

Jane Day daughter of Edward Day of the Water Guard and Agnes Day his wife, aged 13 years, was buried in the church yard of Saint Nicholas, the 16 day of October 1837, by me, Edw. Eyre Maunsell, Vicar of St Nicholas

Decr 26 1837, Rachel Henry wife of Mr David Henry, was interred in the church yard of St Nicholas, aged 34 years. She died on the 24th inst and on the same day Mr John Murphy, brazier, aged 49 years. He died the same day also, H. Morgan

January 24th 1838, Barnaby Middleton was interred by me, in the church yard of Saint Nicholas, aged 77 years, Edw. Eyre Maunsell, Vicar

February 11 1838, John Francis Hutchinson, late Capn of the Galway Volunteers & late Lieut in the Line, was interred in the church yard of Saint Nicholas. He was aged 75 years, Edw. Eyre Maunsell, Vicar, H. Morgan, Vicar

Feby 11 1838, James Beatty, aged 4 years, son of Sergeant Joseph Beatty of Her Majesty's 8th Regt of Foot and of Sarah his wife. He died the 10th inst, H. Morgan, Vicar

[Page] 442

Thomas Collins, drummer in Her Majesty's 8th Regt of Foot, was interred in the church yard on the 24th day of Feby 1838. He died on the 22nd, H. Morgan, Vicar

[Pages 443-472 blank]

[Pages 473-488 are lost]

[Page] 489 [loose]

Interments in the Parish of St Nicholas, Galway
On Saturday Decr 25th 1802 two, Robert McNi[page torn, text lost] [ma]riner late of Belfast, John Campbell, Vicar
Monday Feby 14th 1803 three, Mrs Jane Stedma[n, page torn, text lost]
Tuesday May 27th 1803, Mr George Thomp[son, page torn, text lost] [page torn, text lost] of the 63rd Regt of Foot, Jno. Campbell, Vicar
Tuesday May the 24th 1803,[63] Mr Ambrose Or[page torn, text lost] [page torn, text lost] of Mr James Clarke, Revenue Officer, John Camp[bell]
Sunday August the 28th 1803, Thomas Anderson, shoema[page torn, text lost]
Galway
Theophilus Eaton, Revenue Officer, 26th [June] 1803
Robert Shaw Esqr son of the Revd Robt Shaw – Mrs Shaw of the West
Benjamin Roberts, Novr 4th, a Sergeant of the K[ings] C[ounty] Militia
[Sun]day Novr 24th, Alley Jolly of the West
On Sunday Decr 1st John Bradley of the town of Galway
Robert Squibb [Tues ?] 1805
John Hudson Septr 25th 1806
Martha Shaw daughter of Revd Robt Shaw, Galway, Septr 26th 1806
Tuesday 21st Oct [page torn, text lost] Dodgeworth wife of Luke Dodgeworth [page torn, text lost]
George Whelnal on Monday [remainder of entry is lost]
Decr 22nd 1806 – Captain Jam[remainder of entry is lost]
Monday 29th Decr 1806 [remainder of entry is lost]
[page torn, text lost] wife of Thos Taylor of Dom[remainder of entry is lost]
[page torn, text lost] Thomas of Oranmore, Excise [Officer?, remainder of entry is lost]

---

[63] There is some error in either the days or dates here with reference to Tuesday 27th May and Tuesday 24th May both entered for the same year.

[page torn, text lost] 1823 Capt Trist[ram] [Although the remainder of this entry is lost, it most probably refers to Capt Tristram Carey of the 3rd Royal Veteran Battalion, who died on 24 Dec 1823 and was buried in the graveyard at St Nicholas, see Higgins and Heringklee, *Monuments of St Nicholas Collegiate Church, Galway*. There is also a register index entry for him relating to page 489].

[The register proper ends here. The remaining entries are composed of two loose pages and entries from the index which is at the front of the volume. In the original register the information on these pages is not recorded chronologically, but, for the purposes of this edition, has been reproduced in a chronological form. The numbers in round brackets before each block of entries refer to the page numbers of the original index. The two loose pages are not numbered, and start the sequence].

[Loose page]

Baptisms
May 29th 1800, baptized Simon and Henry twin sons of James Marshall of Kilkerky in the Parish of Rahoon, Robt Shaw, Vicar
June 16th 1800, baptized Anne daughter of Willm Walsh, Royal Irish Artillery in the Parish of St Nicholas, Galway, Robt Shaw, Vicar
July 16th 1800, baptized Catherine daughter of John McGregor of the Glangary Fencible Regiment in the Parish of St Nicholas, Robt Shaw, Vicar
October 5th 1800, baptized Cecilia daughter of John Lord Clanmorris [page torn, text lost] the Parish of Rahoon, John Campbell, Vicar
On Sept 17th 1802, baptized Caphy daughter of Alexr Chisholm, Private of the Reay Re[gt?] Infantry, John [Campbell?]
On Septr 25th 1801, baptized Albert son of George [page torn, text lost]end, Sergeant of the Reay Regt of Fencible Infantry, John Campbell, Vicar
On Septr 26th 1801, baptized Margaret daughter of [page torn, text lost] FitzGibbon of the Royal Irish Artillery, John Campbell, Vicar
[page torn]ber 1[?]th 1801, baptized Elizabeth daughter of [page torn, text lost] of the town of Galway, ropemaker, John Campbell, Vicar
[page torn]ber 31st 180[1] baptized Esthe[page torn, text lost] of the Royal Irish Artillery, John Campell, Vicar

[Loose page]

Bapti[sms]
Saturday April the 10th 1802, baptized Mary daughter of John Morrison, Sergant of the Reay Fencible Regiment, John Campbell, Vicar
Wednesday April 13th 1802, baptized Anne daughter of John Maleod of the Reay Regiment, John Campbell, Vicar
Friday April 16th 1802, baptized George son of William Chisolhme, Corporal of the Reay Regiment, John Campbell, Vicar
Tuesday April 20th 1802, baptized Willm son of John Canty of the town of Galway, cabinet maker. Also on same day William son of Jas Mackey of the Reay Regt quartered here, John Campbell, Vicar
Sunday May 23rd 1802, baptized Mary daughter of William Mackenzie, Private of the Reay Regt, John Campell Vicar
Saturday May 29th 1802, baptized Robert son of John Macullogh, Private of the Reay Regt, Jno. Campbell, Vicar
Sun[day] June 13th 1802 two, baptized Hynacinth [page torn, text lost] Captn Devereux of the Wexford Militia, James Campbell, Vicar
Mon[day] June 14th 1802 two, baptized Robert son of John Campbell, Private of the Reay Regiment, John Campbell, Vicar
Friday July the 16th 1802 two, baptized William son of Thomas Squibb of the town of Galway, John Campbell, Vicar
Thursday July the 22nd 1802 two, baptized [page torn, text lost] son of Dominick Tennant, tidewater [page torn, text lost], John Camp[bell]
Wednesday August the 4th 1802 two, [page torn, text lost] daughter of Richard Pe[ar?] [page torn, text lost], John Cam[pbell?]
August the 9th 1802 [the last entry is lost apart from the date]

(3)

[Friday] August 28th [1802], baptized Catherine [illegible] daughter of Sir John Blake of Menlogh, Bart, John Campbell, Vicar
Sunday Septr 5th 1802 two, baptized Mary daughter of James Leslie, late Sergeant of the Suffolk Regt of Fencibles, John Campbell, Vicar
Sunday Septr 12th 1802 two, baptized Georgina daughter of [name faded, Alexander?] Macartney, Revenue Officer of Galway, John Campbell, Vicar

Friday Septr 17th 1802, baptized Frances daughter of Robert Nicolson, late of the Artillery, John Campbell, Vicar

Friday October 15th 1802, baptized Francis Luke son of George [illegible but probably Connolly] of the town of Galway, stationer, John Campbell, Vicar

Sunday October 24th, baptized James son of Reuben Hughes Esqr, paper manufacturer, John Campbell, Vicar

Saturday Novr 6th 1802, baptized Elizabeth daughter of [Thomas?] Brown Esqr, of Woodstock near Galway, John Campbell, Vicar

Sunday November 28th 1802 two, baptized James son [of Willi?]am Forbes, of the town of Galway, John Campbell, Vicar

Sunday Decr 12th 1802 two, baptized Jane daughter of [John Ma?]xwell, nailor at the west suburbs, John Campbell, Vicar

[Thurs]day Decr 23rd 1802 two, baptized Thomas son of William Macullogh, nailor of Galway, John Campbell, Vicar

Sunday Jany 9th 1803 three, baptized William son of John Comerford, late of the drivers of the Artillery, John Campbell, Vicar

Sunday Jany 16th 1803 three, baptized Elizabeth daughter of Thomas Abbot Esqr, of Lombard Street, Galway, John Campbell, Vicar

Tuesday Jany 25th 1803, baptized Bridget daughter of John Kirby of Galway, shoemaker, John Campbell, Vicar

Thursday Febr 3rd 1803, baptized Nicholas son of Nicholas Lynch Esqr, of Trinidad, John Campbell, Vicar

Monday Febr 14th 1803, baptized Bridget daughter of Whitnale Campbell, shoemaker of Galway, John Campbell, Vicar

Tuesday Febr 15th 1803, baptized James son of James Glyn[n] of the east suburbs, Galway, John Campbell, Vicar

Wednesday Febr 16th 1803, baptized Elizabeth daughter of Edward Murphy, brazier of Galway, John Campbell, Vicar

Thursday Febr 17th 1803, baptized Anne daughter of Benjamin Thomas, shopkeeper of Galway, John Campbel[l]

March 8th 1803 three, James son Jno. Davis, nailer

[final entry on the page is lost except the surname] Simpson

(4)

Saturday May the fourteenth 1803, baptized Samuel son of Samuel Smyth, sailor, John Campbell, Vicar

Thursday May the 19th 1803 three, baptized Margt daughter of Mr Johnson, Quartermaster of the 36th Regt of Foot

Also on same day William son of John Grant, Sergeant of the 36th Regt of Foot, John Campbell, Vicar

Wednesday June the 15th 1803 three, baptized Honor daughter of John Pugh of Galway, John Campbell, Vicar

Friday June the 24th 1803 three, baptized John Adolphus son of Henry Scott of the town of Galway, cabinet maker, John Campbell, Vicar

Tuesday August the 2nd 1803 three, baptized Joseph son of Ralph Walsh Junr of Galway, John Campbell, Vicar

Thursday August the 4th 1803 three, baptized James son of James Cullen of Galway, John Campbell, Vicar

Sunday Septr 25th 1803 three, baptized William son of John Lackey of Galway, ropemaker, John Campbell, Vicar

Sunday October the 16th, baptized Thomas son [of] Samuel Robinson of Galway, taylor, Jn Campbell [Vicar]

Thursday October the 27th 1803, baptized Anne daughter of Thomas Squibb of Galway, John Campbell, Vicar

Sunday Novr 13th 1803 three, baptized Ebenezer James [son] of Captain Ebenezer Hills of Galway, vintner, John Campbell, Vicar

Saturday December 17th 1803 three, baptized Martin son of Mathew Coghlan of Rahoon, John Campbell, Vicar

Sunday December 18th 1803 three, baptized Martha daughter of Dominick Tennant, Revenue Officer, John Campbell, Vicar

Sunday Decembert 25th 1803 three, baptized James Rattry son of [blank] Meartis, servant of General Hill, John Campbell, Vicar

Sunday January the 1st 1804 four, baptized Richard son [of] Richard Jackson, of the 36th Regt of Foot, John Campbell, Vicar

Sunday January the 8th 1804 four, baptized John son of Reuben Hughes, paper manufacturer, Galway, John Campbell, Vicar

Thursday Feby 2nd 1804 four, baptized Thomas son of Sir John Blake of Menlo, Baronet, John Campbell, Vicar

Sunday February 5th 1804 four, baptized Edward son Edward Jones of Newtown Smith, John Campbell, Vicar

Monday February 6th 1804 four, baptized Elizabeth daughter of Andrew Robinson, jeweller, John Campbell, Vicar

Sunday February 12th 1804 four, baptized Henry son [of] Richard Pears, chandler, John Campbell, Vicar

(9)

Thursday February 16th 1804 four, baptized James son of Owen Green, of Kilkenny Militia, John Campbell, Vicar
Sunday February 19th 1804 four, baptized Elizabeth daughter of Robert Marshal, of the Brigade, John Campbell, Vicar
Thursday March 15th, baptized George son of George Simcockes, attorney, Galway, John Campbell, Vicar
Sunday March the 18th 1804 four, baptized Maria daughter of George Connolly of Galway, stationer, John Campbell, Vicar
Monday March 19th 1804 four, baptized Margaret daughter of Doctr Whistler, Staf[f] Surgeon, John Campbell, Vicar
Friday March 30th 1804 four, baptized John son of James Lyons of Daragh, Cunnemara, John Campbell, Vicar
Saturday March 31st 1804 four, baptized Sarah daughter of Christopher Walker, Sergt of Carlow Militia, John Campbell, Vicar
Wednesday May 9th 1804 four, baptized Richard son of James Clarke, Revenue Officer, John Campbell, Vicar
Sunday May 20th 1804 four, baptized Louisa daughter of Benjamin Thomas, Galway, John Campbell, Vicar
Sunday June 24th 1804 four, baptized Robert son of Jackson Ferris, of the Revenue cruizer, John Campbell, Vicar
Sunday July 1st 1804 four, baptized William son Digby Devenish Esqr of Galway, John Campbell, Vicar
Tuesday July 3rd 1804 four, baptized Anne daughter of Joseph Lewis of the West, John Campbell, Vicar
Wednesday July the 18th 1804 four, baptized Clarinda Mary daughter of Richard Jannes, Revenue Officer, John Campbell, Vicar
Sunday August 12th 1804 four, baptized William Nelson of John Maxwell of Galway, nailor, Jno. Campbell, Vicar
Sunday September 16th 1804 four, baptized Elizabeth daughter of Robert Mulhall, Sergt of Artillery Driver[s], John Campbell, Vicar
Thursday Septr 20th 1804 four, baptized John son of James Cullen of Galway, vintner, John Campbell, Vicar
Sunday Septr 23rd 1804 four, baptized Elizabeth daughter of James Irvine, Corporal 21st Regt, John Campbell, Vicar
Sunday October 14th 1804 four, baptized Hannah daughter of James Francis, paper maker, Galway, John Campbell, Vicar

Same day also Martin son of John Pugh of Galway, John Campbell, Vicar

Friday Novr 2nd 1804 four, baptized Nathaniel son of John Taggart, shoemaker of Galway, John Campbell, Vicar

Wednesday December 11th 1805 fove [five], baptized Thomas Richard son of T. [surname illegible and has been crossed out], Galway, same day Thomas son of James Moore, Private of the Louth M[ilitia][64], Galway, John Campbell, Vicar

(10)

Wednesday the ninth day of January 1805 five, baptized Anne daughter of Benjamin Grandy, Sergeant of the 36th Regt of Foot, John Campbell, Vicar

Saturday the nineteenth day of January 1805 five, baptized Thomas son of Thomas Browne Junr of Galway, Barrack Master, John Campbell, Vicar

Sunday January 20th 1805, baptized Richard son of William Blair, Lieut South Cork Militia now quartered in Galway, John Campbell, Vicar

Sunday March 31st 1805, baptized Hannah daughter of Henry Scott of Galway, cabinet maker, Jno. Campbell, Vicar

Monday April 8th 1805 five, baptized Maria Eliza daughter of Thomas Kine of Galway Esqr, John Campbell, Vicar

Wednesday April the 10th 1805, baptized John son of John Clark, Private of Monaghan Militia, Jn Campbell Vicar

Monday May 6th 1805, baptized Jane Margaret daughter of Sir John Blake of Menlo Bart, John Campbell, Vicar

Friday May 10th 1805, baptized William son of George Guthrie of the east suburbs of Galway, cooper, John Campbell, Vicar

Thursday May the 23rd 1805 five, baptized Sabina daughter of Thomas Farrington of Galway, John Campbell, Vicar

Sunday May the 26th 1805, baptized Eleanor daughter of Edward Murphy of Galway, brazier, John Campbell, Vicar

Saturday June the 8th, baptized Frances daughter of George Sterling of Galway, Revenue Officer, John Campbell

---

[64] See the baptismal entry for Thomas Moore dated 9 Dec 1805 on page (2).

Wednesday June 12th 1805, baptized John son of Jas Clark of the town of Galway, Revenue Officer, Jn Campbell Vicar

Sunday June the 23rd 1805 five, baptized John son of George Simcockes of Galway, attorney also same day baptized Christopher son of Digby Devenish of Arran near Galway, John Campbell, Vicar

Sunday June the 2nd 1805 five, baptized John Douglas son of Jno. Coyle, of the 42nd Regt of Highland Foot, John Campbell, Vicar

Sunday July 14th 1805 five, baptized a foundling left on the Parish, with whom there was a label on its breast requesting that the infant should be named Mary Nolan, John Campbell, Vicar

(1)

[text lost], baptized Mary daughter of Samuel Hart[?] Esqr & Surgeon of the Militia Brigade, John Campbell, Vicar

[text lost] 22nd 1805, baptized Edward Emmanuel son of [Charles Bing]ham,[65] town [Major?] of Galway, John Campbell, Vicar

July 26th 1805, baptized Eleanor daughter of Richd Pears of [Galway?], shopkeeper, John Campbell, Vicar

Sunday Septr 15th 1805, baptized John son of Saml Robinson of Galway, taylor, John Campbell, Vicar

Monday Septr 16th 1805, baptized Esther daughter of Raph Welsh of Galway, baker, John Campbell, Vicar

[text faded] 1805, baptized Mary daughter of Michael Smyth of the Galway Regt Militia, John Campbell, Vicar

[Sun]day Sept 22nd 1805, baptized Benjamin son of Nathl Roberts of the west suburbs, Galway, John Campbell, Vicar

Wednesday Sept 25th 1805 five, baptized George son of John Leckey of [page torn, text lost] Galway, ropemaker, John Campbell, Vicar

[text lost] 1805 five, baptized Catharine daughter of [page torn, text lost], Galway, shoemaker, John Campbell, Vicar

[text lost] 28th 1805 five, baptized Meayan daughter of [page torn, text lost] of town of Galway, brewer, John Campbell, Vicar

[text lost] Octr 31st 1805 five, baptized Elizabeth daughter of Dom[inick Tenn]ant of Galway, Revenue Officer, John Campbell, Vicar

---

[65] See baptism of Eleanor Maria Jane daughter of Major Charles Binghm on 21 June 1807 on page (12).

[text lost] November 3rd 1805, baptized Alley daughter of Willm Macullogh of Galway, nailor, John Campbell, Vicar

Wednesday Novr [?] 1805 five, baptized Mathew son of Mathew Coghlan, Parish of Rahoon, John Campbell, Vicar

Saturday Novr 25th 1805 five, baptized Elizabeth daughter of G[illegible] Copper, Private of the King's County Militia, John Campbell, Vicar

Wednesday Novr 27th 1805 five, baptized Thos son of Robt Wigg[er], Private [text lost] Militia, John Campbell, Vicar

[text lost] 1805 five, baptized Thos son of Robt Robinson, of [text lost] of Foot

Do[66] also William son of Henry Bright [after which one line of text is missing]

also same day Anne daughter of John Leckey, [text lost], ropemaker, John Campbell, Vicar

[text lost], baptized Judith daughter of Laurence Simpson of the [illegible] Militia quartered here, John Campbell, Vicar

(2)

Monday the 9th Decr 1805 five, baptized Thomas son of James Moore, Private of Louth Militia, John Campbell, Vicar[67]

Monday 16th Decr 1805, baptized John son of Captain Robert O'Brien, of the Royal Navy, John Campbell, Vicar

Sunday December the 22nd 1805 five, baptized Thomas son of James Barry, Private of the King's County Militia, John Campbell, Vicar

Sunday December 29th 1805 five, baptized John son of Richard O'Connor, Captain of the King's Co Militia, John Campbell, Vicar

Tuesday December 31st 1805 five, baptized Mary daughter of Richard McLean, Sergeant of the King's Co Militia, Jn Campbell Vicar

Sunday Jany 5th 1806 six, baptized John son of Wm McLean, Sergeant of the 92nd Regt, one of the Brigade, John Campbell, Vicar

Saturday Jany 18th 1806 six, baptized Sarah daughter of Pat Moran, of 49th Regt, John Campbell, Vicar

---

[66] Ditto

[67] This child's baptism is entered again on page (9), where the date is given as 11th Dec 1805.

Sunday Jany 19th 1806 six, baptized Eliz[page torn, text lost] James Moody, Sergt of 66th Regt of Foot, Joh[text lost]

Sunday Jany 26th 1806 six, baptized Elizabeth [daughter of] Joseph Maculla of the east suburbs, Galway, John Campbell, [Vicar]

Sunday Feby 10th 1806 six, baptized David son of David Barry of the West of Galway, nailor, John Campbell, Vicar

Monday Feby 11th 1806 six, baptized Mary, a Parish child found on Saturday night, John Campbell, Vicar

Friday the eighth day of March 1806 six, baptized Thomas son of Henry Scott of Galway, cabinet maker, John Campbell, Vicar

Thursday March 13th 1806 six, baptized Charles son of Charles Bell, Corporal of the 92nd Light Company, John Campbell, Vicar

Monday March 17th 1806 six, baptized Alexand[page torn, text lost] William Hunter, of the 92nd Light Company, John C[page torn, text lost]

Wednesday March 19th 1806 six, baptized Elizabe[th] daughter of Richd Knowles, 36th Regt, Jno. Campbell

(11)

Sunday April 6th 1806 six, baptized the following infants Mary daughter of John Smith, 89th Regt of Foot. Marian daughter of Jn McIntosh, Staff Sergeant, John Campbell, Vicar

Monday April 7th 1806, baptized Joseph son of Wm Bernan, Corporal of the 92nd Regt of Foot, John Campbell, Vicar

Wednesday April 16th 1806, baptized Honoria Catharine daughter of William Blair, Lieut of the S. Cork Militia, John Campbell, Vicar

Sunday April 27th 1806, baptized Catherine daughter of Andrew Robinson of Galway, jeweller, John Campbell, Vicar

Saturday May 17th 1806, baptized Mary daughter of Thomas Browne, Barrack Master of Galway also on same [day] Reuben son of Reuben Hughes of Galway, paper manufacturer at Dominick St, John Campbell, Vicar

Thursday May 29th 1806 six, baptized Thomas son of Thomas Abbott of the Salmor Were [Salmon Weir], John Campbell, Vicar

Sunday June 1st 1806 six, baptized Jane daughter of James Francis of the West, John Campbell, Vicar

Sunday June 29th 1806, baptized John son of John Davis of the west suburbs, nailor, John Campbell, Vicar
Sunday July [no day] 1806 six, baptized Eliza daughter of Jno. Griffith of the town of Galway, shoemaker, John Campbell, Vicar
Sunday Septr 14th 1806, baptized Mary daughter of George Wheeler of Galway, ropemaker, John Campbell, Vicar
Sunday Septr 28th 1806, baptized a Parish foundling by name Michael, John Campbell, Vicar
Wednesday October 29th 1806 six, baptized John son of Robert Mulholland, Sergeant of the Drivers Corp, John Campbell, Vicar
Monday Novr 18th 1806 six, baptized John son of Ralph Walsh Junior of Galway, baker, John Campbell, Vicar
Friday Dec 26th 1806, baptized Willm Patrick son of Peter Willian, Lieut of R[oyal] Navy, Jno. Campbell, Vicar
Thursday Jany 5th 1807 seven, baptized Alexander William son of Duncan Cameron of Eyreville near Galway, this child was born 29th Nov 1806, Jno. Campbell, Vicar

(12)

Saturday Jany 14th 1807 seven, baptized Anne daughter of Richard Pear of Galway, sailmaker, John Campbell, Vicar
Monday Jany 19th 1807 seven, baptized John son John Cox of the town of Galway, shoemaker, John Campbell, Vicar
Sunday February 8th 1807 seven, baptized Henry son of Henry Scott of Galway, cabinet maker, John Campbell, Vicar
Sunday February the 15th 1807, Lucius son of Captain Robt O'Brien of the Royal Navy was baptized by Rev L.H.Young
Friday February 27th, baptized Mary daughter of John Lackey of the West, Galway, ropemaker, Jno. Campbell, Vicar [double signature possibly to verify previous entry]
Monday March 30th 1807 seven, baptized John Charles son of Digby Devenish of Arran Esqr, Jno. Campbell, Vicar
Thursday June 4th 1807 seven, baptized Isabella daughter of Sir Jno. Blake of Menlo Bt, John Campbell, Vicar
Sunday June 7th 1807 seven, baptized Maria daughter of Thomas Farrington of the west suburbs, Galway, John Campbell, Vicar

Friday June 12th 1807 seven, baptized John son of Domk Tennant of Galway, Revenue Officer, John Campbell, Vicar

Sunday June 21st 1807 seven, baptized Eleanor Maria Jane daughter of Major Charles Bingham of Galway, Jno. Campbell, Vicar

Monday June 22nd 1807, baptized Letitia daughter of Andrew Robinson of Galway, jeweller, John Campbell, Vicar

Sunday June 28th 1807, baptized Samuel son of Saml Robinson of Galway, taylor, John Campbell, Vicar

Sunday July 5th 1807, baptized Isabella daughter of Wm Mason, one of the sheriffs of Galway, John Campbell, Vicar

Monday July 6th 1807, baptized Margaret daughter of M. Farrell, of the 101st Regt of Foot now on foreign service, John Campbell, Vicar

Sunday July 19th 1807 seven, baptized John son of Jesse Shaw of Galway, cabinet maker, John Campbell, Vicar

Sunday Septr 27th 1807, baptized Eliza daughter of Wm Forbes of the east suburbs of Galway, John Campbell, Vicar

Friday Dec 18th 1807 seven, baptized Isabella daughter of John Darcy of [illegible], John Campbell, Vicar

Sunday Jany 10th 1808, baptized Mary Anne daughter of Joseph Lewis of the west suburbs, John Campbell, Vicar

Friday Jany 22nd 1808, baptized John son of Patrick Hearn of the town of Galway, shoemaker, John Campbell, Vicar

Sunday Jany [no day] 1808, baptized John son of Wm Wheeler of the Green, ropemaker, John Campbell, Vicar

Brought forward to page 15   [Baptisms continue on page 15 of the register]

(5)

[The index begins on this page with the letter 'B'. In the middle of the page there is an original entry, as reproduced here:]

Bequest of the late Mrs Halliday was left to the poor of the church of St Nicholas Galway which donation is to be distributed half yearly viz Christmas & Easter to 24 on the money list – two pounds ten shillings at these two periods. The sum total being five pounds yearly arising from a house in Whitehall in the town of Galway. The present tenant in possession being one Ulick Burke a carpenter now living in Galway. John Campbell, Vicar.

(6)

Sunday January 19th 1812, baptized John Foster son of Richard Pears of Bridge Street, Galway, John Campbell, Vicar

Thursday Jan 23rd 1812, Henry Harms of the Parish of Oranmore in the Wardenship of Galway and Anne Manhal of the Parish of Rahoon spinster, were joined together in holy matrimony in the church of St Nicholas, Galway, John Campbell, Vicar

Thursday February 30th 1812, baptized Hariot daughter of Henry Scott of Galway, cabinet maker, John Campbell, Vicar

Sunday May 24th 1812, baptized John son of George Macartney of Galway, musician, also same day Mary, a Parish child, John Campbell, Vicar

Tuesday June 2nd 1812, baptized William son of Patrick Hearn of Galway, shoemaker, John Campbell, Vicar

Sunday June 25th 1812, baptized Mary daughter of Wm Mason, one of the sheriffs of the town of Galway, John Campbell, Vicar

Saturday July 4th 1812, baptized William son of Reuben Hughes of Galway, John Campbell, Vicar

Monday July 6th 1812, baptized Robert son of Duncan Cameron Esqr of Galway

Tuesday July 7th 1812, baptized Mary daughter of John Cox of Galway, shoemaker, John Campbell, Vicar

Tuesday August 4th 1812, baptized George son of Jno. Storey of Galway, sailmaker, John Campbell, Vicar

Sunday August 16th 1812, baptized Archibald son of Capt MacDorig, Adjutant of the Argyleshire Militia, John Campbell, Vicar

(14)

Edward Milway & Rachel Hodgins married by regular licence at canonical hours, on the 11th of February 1814, by me, James Daly
Witness David Smyth

John Ryan & Bridget Gill married after banns duly published at ten o'clock, Decr 29th, by me, James Daly, Minister
Witnesses James Ryan, John Moran

Feby 8th 1817, James Buchanan & Catharine Furlong by licence from his Grace the Archbishop of Tuam, by permission, John Whitley
Witness John Stedman

(15)

Elisha Brigg and Margarette Monaghan married, after banns duly published, by me, H. Morgan, Decr 28th 1819
Michael Brennan and Anne Burke married, after banns duly published, by me, H. Morgan, Decr 28th 1819

(19)

Decemr 7th 1818, married Wm Carder to Jane Bartlett by publication [of banns], John Whitley, G[arriso]n Chaplain
Jno. Steadman

(26) [under F]

Funerals [There is actually only one funeral entry]

June 15th 1800, buried in the church yard of Galway, Catherine Strogen wife of Samuel Strogen of the town of Galway, Robt Shaw, Vicar
Michael Flahertie was admitted into the Church of England by law established having performed all the requisites, on Thursday March 4th 1810, in the Parish Church of St Nicholas, Galway, by John Campbell, Vicar

(32) [under H]

James Humphreys son of Henry & Margaret Humphreys, of the 22nd Regimt, was baptized here, on the 18th of January 1793, by the Revd Mr Gardiner

(37)   [under K]

This is to certify that Patrick Kelly & Sarah Burke were married by me, after banns duly published, in the Church of St Nicholas, Galway,

May 11 1814, by me, James Daly
Witness [blank]
This is to certify that I married Anthony Keevers & Elizabeth Bates, on the 26th of Dec 1819, H. Morgan

(42)   [under M]

Married on Saturday the 20th of July 1816, Robert Hedges Maunsell Esq. to Miss E. Dorothea Maunsell, in the Church of Galway at the hour of 9 o'clock, by me, Geo. Maunsell, Dean of Leighlin
Present John Steadman, Parish Clarke

(46)   [under N]

I certify that Master Jack F[ochea]d & Bridget Moran were married in Church, this 13th of [illegible], by me, Edwd Burke, Vicar of Galway

(50)   [under P]

I hereby certify that John Parry & Honor Healy were married by me, July 15 1816, by banns, James Daly, Minister

(65)   [under W]

James Wright to Mary Lord by publication [of banns], 1st Decemr 1818, J. Whitley
John Steadman
Joseph Logan to Anne Candy by licence from the Archbishop of Tuam, January 16th 1819, John Whitley

(66)

October 26th 1816, Seregeant [sic] Gabriel Wallace of the 2nd Battalion of 12th Regt of Foot, was married to Elizabeth Joyce of Galway, spinster, by the Revd Robert Shaw, one of the Vicars of Galway and Garrison Chaplain, John Campbell, Vicar of Galway

August 24th 1817, Charles William son of Gabriel Wallace, Sergeant of 2nd Battalion 12th Regt of Foot, was baptized by the Revd Robert Shaw etc etc [sic], John Campbell, Vicar

Appendix A

A list of regiments of the British Army and Militia stationed in Galway based on information from the register of baptisms, marriages and burials of St Nicholas's parish, 1792-1840.

56th Regiment 1792, 1811
27th Regiment of Foot 1792
39th Regiment of Foot 1792-3
Tyrone Militia 1794-5, 1811
Northampton Regiment of Fencibles 1795
Downshire Militia 1797
Kerry Militia 1798
Perthshire Regiment of Fencibles 1798
Suffolk Regiment of Fencibles 1798-1800
Wicklow Militia 1800
Carabineers 1800
Waterford Militia 1800
Royal Irish Artillery 1800-1
Glangary Regiment of Fencibles 1800
9th Regiment of Light Dragoons 1801
South Cork Militia 1801-2 & 1805-6
62nd Regiment 1801
Reay Regiment of Fencibles 1801-2
Suffolk Regiment of Fencibles 1802
36th Regiment of Foot 1802-6
Kilkenny Militia 1804
Carlow Militia 1804
17th Regiment of Light Dragoons 1804
25th Regiment of Foot 1804
King's County Militia 1805, 1814
Louth Militia 1805
Monaghan Militia 1805
42nd Regiment of Highland Foot 1805
Sligo Militia 1805
92nd Regiment (Light Company) 1806
49th Regiment 1806
66th Regiment of Foot 1806
89th Regiment of Foot 1806
26th Regiment of Foot 1806
28th Regiment of Foot (1st Battalion) 1806

88th Regiment of Foot 1808, 1814
7th Garrison Battalion 1808
53rd Regiment of Foot 1809
51st Regiment of Foot 1810
Tipperary Militia 1810-1, 1815
Argyleshire Militia 1812
Westmoreland Militia 1813
Berkshire Militia 1814
74th Regiment of Foot 1814-5
12th Regiment of Foot (2nd Battalion) 1816-7
77th Regiment of Foot 1820
9th Veteran Battalion 1820
57th Regiment 1821-2
43rd Regiment of Foot 1822
3rd Royal Veteran Battalion 1822-3, 1825
1st Royal Veteran Battalion 1824-6
22nd Regiment of Foot 1826, 1836
17th Regiment of Foot 1827
34th Regiment of Foot 1828, 1832
64th Regiment of Foot 1828-9, 1833
75th Regiment of Foot 1829
5th Regiment of Foot 1829-30, 1832
Royal Engineers 1829, 1832
28th Regiment of Foot 1831
68th Regiment (Light Infantry) 1832
67th Regiment 1832-3
30th Regiment of Foot 1833-4
82nd Regiment 1834
85th Regiment of Foot (Light Infantry) 1834-5
30th Regiment of Foot 1834-5
78th Highland Infantry 1836
15th Regiment of Foot 1836-7
18th (Royal Irish) Regiment of Foot 1836-7
8th Regiment 1837-8

Appendix B

Biographical notes on the clergy of the parish of St Nicholas, Galway, in chronological order, 1792-1840

Drelincourt Young Campbell, vicar c. 1792-1799

The Revd D.Y. Campbell was the son of Dr John Campbell, vicar general of Tuam, and his wife, a Miss Young. Dr Campbell died in 1772, aged 47, and was buried in Tuam.[68] His son Drelincourt Campbell entered T.C.D. on 8 July 1762, became a scholar in 1765, graduating with a B.A. in 1767. In 1768 on the recommendation of his cousin, the Revd James Drought, he was appointed master of the Erasmus Smith school in Galway. He had a successful career at the school and sometime before 1792 was also made a vicar of the collegiate church of St Nicholas.[69] Campbell attended meetings of Galway corporation as a burgess from 1770, and at a public assembly at the Tholsel on 24 May 1777, his application to be elected as a free burgess was unanimously agreed by members of the corporation. His signature is appended to the minutes of a meeting of the corporation on 30 May 1777.[70] He died on 5 August 1799, and his wife Sarah died on 20 April 1822, aged 74. Both are buried in St Nicholas's graveyard.

Some colourful stories have been written about the descent of the Revd D.Y. Campbell's maternal ancestors - the Youngs - from Louis XIV and the Comtesse de Montmorenci, especially in books about the explorer Sir Richard Burton, who was a cousin.[71] The most plausible account of the French royal connection is provided in MacDonnell's *Some notes on the Graves family* (Dublin 1889). According to this source, the daughter of Henri, Duke de Montmorenci, lord high

---

[68] Higgins and Parsons, *St Mary's cathedral*, p. 109.
[69] Michael Quane, 'Galway Grammar School', in *JGAHS*, xxxi (1964), pp. 39-70, gives a detailed account of Revd D.Y. Campbell's time as master of the Erasmus Smith school.
[70] Galway Corporation Records, Liber K1 p. 52.
[71] Georgina M. Stisted *The true life of Capt Sir Richard F. Burton* (1896), Hercules Henry Graves MacDonnell, *Some notes on the Graves family* (Dublin 1889).

admiral of France (and later executed in 1632), had married a Hugenot named Hercules Le Jeune. The sister of Hercules Le Jeune married the Revd Peter Drelincourt, who fled France for Holland, after the revocation of the Edict of Nantes in 1685. Drelincourt eventually ended up in Ireland and after a succession of clerical appointments was made dean of Armagh in 1691.[72] Hercules Le Jeune had had a son Louis Henry, whom he sent to Holland about 1700. This son moved on to stay with his maternal uncle, the dean at Armagh, and changed his name from Le Jeune to Young. A daughter of Louis Henry Young married Dr John Campbell and they were the parents of Revd D.Y. Campbell. The gravestone of a Revd Lewis Henry Young lies beside the gravestone of the Revd D.Y. Campbell and his wife Sarah in St Nicholas's graveyard. The Revd L.H. Young came to Galway in the mid-1780s, to serve as usher at the Erasmus Smith school where his cousin, the Revd D.Y. Campbell, was master. He was the son of Drelingcourt Young, born in county Wicklow *c.* 1761. He entered T.C.D. in 1775, became a scholar in 1778, and graduated with a B.A. in 1779. At the time of his death on 9 June 1815, he was serving as rector of Kilcolgan, county Galway. His gravestone was erected by his widow Margaret. The Revd L.H. Young is mentioned three times in the register of St Nicholas's between 1792 and 1840. He baptised two of the children of Captain Robert O'Brien, of the Royal Navy, in 1807 and 1808 and he presided over the marriage ceremony of the Revd Thomas Wade, master of the Erasmus Smith school, with Sarah Hamilton on 20 March 1808. The Revd Thomas Wade succeeded the Revd D.Y. Campbell as master of the school in 1800.

Revd Robert Shaw(e), vicar *c.* 1792-1817

The Revd Robert Shaw held the prebend of Ballysadare, in the diocese of Achonry between 1772 and his death in 1817. Concurrently he served as one of the vicars of Galway from at least 1792 (possibly earlier) until 1817. The register records some eleven ceremonies performed by him during this 25-year period. Robert Shaw was educated by a Revd Mr Vesey, before entering T.C.D. in 1763, becoming a scholar in 1765 and graduating with a B.A. in 1767. In 1816 an entry in the register records Shaw as both vicar and chaplain

---

[72] James B. Leslie, *Armagh clergy and parishes* (Dundalk, 1911), pp. 19-20.

of the garrison.[73]. He married Susanna Lea of St Mark's parish, Dublin, in 1769. She died on 29 May 180(0?), aged 54 and was buried in St Nicholas's graveyard with two of their children, Robert, who died in 1803, and Martha, who died in 1806 aged 23.[74] The Revd Robert Shaw died in 1817.

John Campbell, vicar 1799-1818

The Revd John Campbell served as a vicar of St Nicholas's between 1799 and 1818. He was the son of the above Revd Drelincourt Campbell. Born in Galway, he entered T.C.D. on 22 October 1787 aged 18, graduating with a B.A. in 1792. Like his father, Campbell junior regularly attended common council meetings of the Galway corporation. He died on 13 March 1818, aged 46 and is buried in St Nicholas's graveyard.[75] The *Galway Express* later recorded the death of his widow, Alicia, at Mitchelstown, county Cork, on 7 March 1862. She was the third daughter of Henry Sadlier of Cork.[76]

James Daly, warden 1811-64

The Revd James Daly was born in county Galway on 12 March 1790.[77] He was the son of the Revd Ralph Daly who served as warden of Galway between 1786 and 1810. James Daly was a first cousin of James Daly, the first Baron Dunsandle and Clanconal. He entered T.C.D. on 3 October 1803 aged 16, and was awarded a B.A. in 1808.

---

[73] See page (66) at the end of the register.
[74] J. B. Leslie, Biographical succession list of the clergy of the diocese of Achonry, RCB Library, MS 61/2/9, p. 23; Higgins and Heringklee, *Monuments of St Nicholas collegiate church*, p. 15, and also p. 489 of the register.
[75] There appears to be some inconsistency about his age, perhaps he was aged 48 at the time of his death, see Higgins and Heringklee, *Monuments of St Nicholas collegiate church*, p. 82.
[76] *Galway Express*, 15 March 1862.
[77] His gravestone inscription as published in Higgins and Heringklee, *Monuments of St Nicholas collegiate church,* p. 66, states he was born in 1790, while the *Alumni Dublinensis* records that he entered T.C.D. in 1803 aged 16.

He succeeded his father as warden of Galway in 1811.[78] He married Jemima daughter of Thomas Browne of Moyne, near Monivea, county Galway, in St Nicholas's church on 21 February 1826. They lived in a house known as 'the Villa' in Galway. The vestry minutes of a meeting held on 7 May 1822 record an acknowledgement of thanks to Daly as warden for his relief of distress during the year 1822.[79] The Revd James Daly died on 6 January 1864, at the age of 75, and was buried in the graveyard of St Nicholas's. Following his death the position of warden was dissolved and instead a rector was appointed (see entry for John D'Arcy below). His wife Jemima who was born on 29 January 1800, died on 6 December 1874, and was buried alongside her husband.[80] The Revd James Daly's sister-in-law, Elizabeth Browne, married the Revd Daniel Foley on 31 August 1820. Foley had been appointed usher at the Erasmus Smith school in 1815 and he conducted a few ceremonies recorded in the register of St Nicholas. He and his wife Elizabeth lived in a house called Averard in Galway. She predeceased him on 9 April 1863, aged 60, while Foley died on 5 April 1876, at the age of 86. Both are buried in St Nicholas's graveyard alongside Elizabeth's parents and sisters.

Revd John Whitley, master of the Erasmus Smith school 1815-37, & garrison chaplain

The Revd John Whitley was born in county Monaghan and entered T.C.D. in January 1801, aged 17. He became a scholar in 1805 and a doctor of divinity in 1822. He was appointed master of the Erasmus Smith school in 1815, and later served as the chaplain to the garrison in Galway barracks.[81] The baptisms of six of Whitley's children (which took place between 1819 and 1833) were entered together in one block on the same page of the register following the baptism of his son Charles in 1833.[82] Another son John later entered T.C.D. in 1841, aged 17. At the Easter general vestry meeting of the parish of

---

[78] Galway Corporation Records, Liber K1.
[79] Vestry minute book of St Nicholas, Galway 1805-1910.
[80] Her gravestone appears to be incorrectly inscribed 1875, see Higgins and Heringklee, *Monuments of St Nicholas collegiate church, Galway,* pp. 66 & 68.
[81] Quane, 'Galway Grammar School'.
[82] See p. 127 of the register.

St Nicholas held in April 1816, a written request from the Revd John Whitley was considered regarding a pew in the church for the accommodation of the pupils of the Erasmus Smith school. As a result, a pew was allocated to the school in May 1816. However numbers at the school declined in the 1830s and Whitley resigned in 1837.

Revd Edward Bourke, vicar *c.* 1818-61

The Revd Edward Bourke was born *c.* 1792. His name appears in the register between the years 1818 and 1835 and is spelt Burke in the earlier entries and Bourke in the later ones. In 1829 he was reprimanded by the grand jury of Galway for a three-year absence from his post as Protestant chaplain to the town gaol.[83] He was more diligent in parish affairs, and the vestry minute book records that he acted as chairman of vestry meetings in the years 1833-1835, 1840 and 1844. The Revd Edward Bourke was recorded as one of the vicars of Galway in the parliamentary return of 1837, and as the senior vicar when he died at 4 Pembroke Place, Dublin, on 11 May 1861, aged 69.[84]

Henry Morgan, vicar 1818-40

The Revd Henry Morgan was the seventh son of Charles Morgan of Monksfield, in the parish of Killogilleen, county Galway. Born in Galway, educated by a Mr FitzGerald, he entered T.C.D. in June 1811 aged 17, graduating with a B.A. in 1815. On 1 January 1828, he married Ellen Davis in St Nicholas's.[85] Five of their children were baptised in the parish between the years 1828 and 1838. His gravestone states that he inherited the family estates in county Galway on the death of his elder brother. He died on 25 May 1840, aged 43.

---

[83] Kennedy, 'The county of the town of Galway', in *JGAHS* (1962-1963), pp. 90-101.
[84] Leslie, Biographical succession list Tuam, RCB Library MS 61/2/15, p. 188.
[85] This event is recorded on p. 73 of the regiser.

Revd John D'Arcy, vicar 1821-64

The Revd John D'Arcy was born *c.* 1793 in county Mayo, the son of John D'Arcy, a lawyer. He was educated first by a Mr Moore, and then entered T.C.D. in 1810 at the age of 16 and obtained a B.A. in 1817 and a M.A. in 1832. He served as a vicar of Galway from 1821-1864, and then became the parish's first rector following the death of the last warden, Revd James Daly, in 1864, a position in which he continued until retirement in 1872. D'Arcy was connected with several urban improvements in Galway during the 50 years he lived in the town, including the establishment of a savings bank, a mendicity institution and a grammar school. He was especially prominent in organising relief during the famine years, 1845-48. According to the register he was married in St Nicholas's on 17 May 1834 to Isabella Elizabeth Reilly, daughter of John Lushington Reilly esq. of Scarvagh House, county Down, who held the post of comptroller of customs in Galway. The couple lived in a house known as the 'Vicar's Croft' in the parish of Rahoon. Three of their children were baptised in the parish in 1835, 1837 and 1839, events also recorded in the register. D'Arcy was living at Prospect Hill, Galway, when he died on 2 September 1875, at the age of 82. He was buried in the graveyard at St Nicholas's. His wife Isabella, who was born in 1808, lived until her ninetieth year, dying in 1898.[86]

Edward Eyre Maunsell, vicar *c.* 1833-64

The Revd Edward Eyre Maunsell was the fifth son of the Revd George Maunsell, rector of Drumcree, in the diocese of Armagh between 1781 and 1804, and later dean of Leighlin, 1804-22. His mother was Helena Hedges Eyre of Macroom castle, county Cork. According to Leslie, Maunsell was born in county Limerick, and first educated by a Mr White before entering T.C.D. in 1804 at the age of just 14. He had obtained a B.A. by 1810 and an M.A. in 1827. He was ordained in 1829,[87] and soon afterwards became a vicar of

---

[86] Higgins and Heringklee, *Monuments of St Nicholas collegiate church*, p. 230.
[87] Leslie, Biographical succession list for the diocese of Tuam, 1938, RCB Library MS 61/2/15, p. 188a.

Galway,[88] where he had been living for sometime, and in which parish he had served as churchwarden in 1815. In 1818 he married Eliza Maria, daughter of Thomas Studdert of Bunratty castle, county Clare and they had one daughter and four sons. Two of their sons were baptised in St Nicholas's in 1830 and 1832. The family lived at Fort Eyre, Shantalla, Galway. Maunsell died on 3 April 1864.[89]

---

[88] Although the register records ceremonies performed by him from 1830, he is not referred to as 'vicar' until July 1833, see page 123 of the register.

[89] Leslie, Biographical succession list for the diocese of Tuam, RCB Library MS 61/2/15, p. 188a.

Bibliography

Primary Sources

St Nicholas's collegiate church, Galway:

>Vestry minute book of St Nicholas, Galway 1805-1910

Representative Church Body Library, Dublin:

>J.B. Leslie (ed.), Biographical succession list for the diocese of Tuam, unpublished typescript, 1938, MS 61/2/15
>J.B. Leslie (ed.), Biographical succession list for the diocese of Achonry, unpublished typescript, 1938, MS 61/2/9.
>Combined register of baptisms, marriages and burials, St Nicholas' collegiate church, Galway, 1792-1840, P.519.1.1

James Hardiman Library Archives, N.U.I.G.:

>Galway Corporation Records Liber K1

Secondary sources

John Andrews, *Plantation acres: an historical study of the Irish land surveyor and his maps* (Belfast, 1985)
Burke's family records (London, 1976)
Burke's landed gentry of Ireland (London, 1871)
G. D. Burtchaell & T. U. Sadlier, *Alumni Dublinensis* (London, 1924)
J. Fleetwood Berry, *The story of St Nicholas' collegiate church, Galway* (Galway, 1912)
James Hardiman, *The history of the town and county of the town of Galway* (Dublin, 1820, & revised edition, Galway, 1985)
G. A. Hayes McCoy, 'Three Galway ships', in *JGAHS,* xxviii (1958-59), pp 1-4
Jim Higgins & Susanne Heringklee (eds.), *Monuments of St Nicholas' collegiate church, Galway* (Galway, 1992)

Jim Higgins & Aisling Parsons (eds.), *St Mary's cathedral (Church of Ireland) Tuam. An architectural, archaeological and historical guide* (Galway, 1995)

Susan Hood (ed.), *Register of the parish of Holy Trinity (Christ Church), Cork, 1643-1669* (Dublin, 1998)

Richard J. Kelly, 'The wardenship of Galway', in *JGAHS,* vi (1909-10), pp 27-33 & 110-122

Patrick J. Kennedy, 'The county of the town of Galway', in *JGAHS,* xxx (1962-63), pp 90-101

James B. Leslie, *Armagh clergy and parishes* (Dundalk, 1911)

Samuel Lewis, *Topographical dictionary of Ireland*, 2 vols (London 1837)

Hercules Henry Graves MacDonnell, *Some notes on the Graves family* (Dublin, 1889)

Anne M. A. Mannion, *The social geography of the British Army in nineteenth-century Ireland with specific reference to Galway,* (unpublished MA thesis, U.C.G., 1994)

Peadar O'Dowd, *Galway city* (Galway, 1998)

M. D. O'Sullivan, *Old Galway. The history of a Norman colony in Ireland* (Cambridge, 1942)

J. Pigot, *City of Dublin and Hibernian provincial directory* (Dublin, 1824)

Michael Quane, 'Galway Grammar School', in *JGAHS,* xxxi (1964-65), pp 39-70

Raymond Refaussé (ed.), *Register of the parish of St Thomas, Dublin, 1750-1791* (Dublin, 1994)

J. G. Simms 'Connacht in the eighteenth century', in *Irish Historical Studies*, xi (1958), pp 116-133

Isaac Slater, *A national, topographical and commercial directory of Ireland* (London, 1856)

Georgina M. Stisted, *The true life of Captain Sir Richard F. Burton* (London, 1896)

Paul Walsh, *Discover Galway* (Dublin, 2001)

Index of surnames

Abbot	131
Abbott	99, 137
Adams	35, 110, 119
Adamson	85
Aiken	91
Albut	74
Allen	63, 104
Allsop	76
Anderson	53, 68, 85, 102, 118, 128
Armstrong	100, 110, 126
Ashe	77
Aspin	65
Atkins	58
Atkinson	72
Atkison	28
Austin	43
Baird	95
Bakehar	29
Baldwin	30
Balford	83
Bankes	33, 122
Banks	102
Barlow	61, 119
Barnard	66
Barnet	87
Barnshaw	93
Barr	67
Barry	25, 53, 58, 98, 102, 136, 137
Barter	95
Bartlett	141
Bates	142
Bath	42
Bayley	71, 87
Bayly	113
Beard	105
Beasmore	73
Beatty	64, 70, 105, 127
Bebbs	36
Beere	105
Behun	51
Bell	51, 119, 137
Bellew	35
Bentley	107
Bently	60, 61, 94, 102
Benton	65, 92, 116
Bernan	137
Berry	81, 97, 99, 102
Biggs	111
Bingham	25, 27, 32, 135, 139
Binns	71
Birchen	43
Bird	69
Birmingham	70
Black	58, 62, 69
Blackburn	92
Blair	32, 36, 102, 122, 134, 137
Blake	24, 25, 27, 28, 29, 30, 34, 35, 38, 40, 41, 45, 55, 59, 60, 74, 76, 82, 85, 86, 92, 93, 108, 112, 117, 118, 130, 132, 134, 138
Blakely	102
Blakeney	61
Blakeny	122, 123, 124
Bloxham	90, 97
Boilean	72
Boland	65
Booth	99, 107
Borradaele	48
Bouchis	51
Bourke	58
Revd Edward	50, 51, 61, 62, 65, 66, 79, 81, 82, 84, 85, 90, 91, 94, 95, 96, 97, 98, 105, 107, 108, 109, 111, 112, 114, 116, 117, 119, 125, 126, 142
Bowden	93
Bowles	68
Boyd	50, 73, 80, 97
Boyle	71
Bradley	42, 124, 128
Bradly	122, 123
Brakley	90
Brandish	87
Brandon	74
Brearly	49
Bredun	122
Brennan	30, 141
Brew	69, 78
Bricknell	86, 118
Brigg	141
Bright	36, 39, 41, 45, 48, 59, 63, 67, 89, 98, 109, 118, 136
Briscoe	110
Briscoh	94
Britton	68
Broad	53
Brooke	75, 78
Brookes	103
Brooks	33
Brown	30, 51, 82, 108, 131

Browne ..24, 32, 48, 54, 56, 58, 66, 68, 72, 78, 80, 81, 85, 86, 95, 105, 110, 115, 118, 134, 137
Bruce 70
Bruway 82
Bryce 35
Buchanan.. 141
Buchannan.. 33
Buck 96
Buckley 123
Buckly 123
Buclscenis 91
Bulger 41
Burdge 66, 74, 80, 92, 96, 97, 101, 108
Burge 76
Burgess 100
Burk 34, 35, 72, 80, 112
Burke 24, 25, 27, 31, 32, 35, 40, 53, 56, 60, 72, 74, 76, 77, 80, 99, 110, 139, 141, 142
Burns 56, 119
Bursteed.. 47
Burton 55
Bust 88
Butler 28, 52, 62, 66, 68, 69, 72, 92, 106
Buttery 126
Button 69
Bynan 55
Byrne 35, 54, 56
Caddy 29, 30, 41, 43, 44, 54, 61, 63, 65, 73, 74, 79, 81, 82, 83, 85, 86, 94, 95, 96, 98, 99, 100, 101, 102, 105, 106, 107, 108, 109, 110, 111, 112, 115, 116, 117, 118, 119, 120, 124
Cahil 26, 27
Calcut 58
Calcutt 96, 100
Callinan 71
Callow 126
Cameron ... 28, 36, 38, 44, 48, 53, 138, 140
Campbell 24, 33, 72, 87, 93, 119, 130, 131
    Revd Drelincourt Young 24, 25, 26, 27, 28, 29
    Revd John..... 29, 30, 31, 32, 33, 34, 35, 36, 37, 38, 39, 40, 41, 42, 43, 44, 45, 46, 47, 48, 49, 128, 129, 130, 131, 132, 133, 134, 135, 136, 137, 138, 139, 140, 141, 143
Canavan.. 30
Candy 142
Cannavan.. 32
Canty 130
Carder.. 141
Carey 54, 57, 129
Carpenter.. 55

Carr 68, 70, 75, 94, 95, 102, 103, 105, 122
Carrick 32, 64
Carson.. 35
Carter 26, 28, 52, 58, 72
Carthy 48
Cartiatt 61
Carty 74
Case 122
Casey 119
Cashel 67, 78, 88
Cashell 55, 58, 85
Cassidy 105
Caulfield 95, 110, 111
Cavanagh 75
Chalkner 55
Chalmers.. 30
Chambers......................... 75, 78, 81, 94
Chester.. 71, 75
Chesterten.. 101
Chevers 81
Cheverson.. 25
Chirm... 113
Chisholm 129
Chislett 47
Chisolhme... 130
Chisolm 111
Christie 29
Church 72
Clancy 91
Clanmorris, Lord 129
Clark 134, 135
Clarke 54, 56, 119, 128, 133
Claxton 106
Clayton 92
Clifford 30
Clinch 25
Cockerall 119
Cody 120
Coffey 57, 58, 66, 79, 88, 93
Coghlan 59, 122, 132, 136
Colahan.. 96
Cole 45, 47, 50
Coleman 117
Colles 60
Collins 112, 115, 127
Collis 114
Comber 67
Comerford 131
Compton 57, 63, 70
Comyns.. 28
Concannon....................................... 32, 84
Conneely 47, 96
Connel 93, 110
Connell 58, 95, 110, 125
Connolly 30, 62, 131, 133

Connor 114
Conolly 37, 42, 60, 102
Considine 52, 73
Conway 65
Cooke 53
Copeland 84
Copland 90, 126
Corbett 39
Cork 64
Cormick 30, 108
Cornvill 71
Costello 76, 79, 124
Cotter 115
Cottingham 24, 35
Coughlan 59, 87
Cox ..27, 28, 29, 33, 34, 35, 38, 57, 59, 84, 86, 102, 123, 138, 140
Coyle 135
Craig 76
Crane 118
Crawford 29, 73
Creuston 37
Crofton 94, 115
Cross 119
Croughan 53
Crowe 53
Crudgeen 102
Cubbage 50
Cudden 69
Cullen 50, 65, 102, 115, 116, 132, 133
Cullin 65
Cunningham 33
Cuppadge 45
Cuppaidge 46, 60
Currie 57
Curry 57
Curtin 109
Cusack 102
D'Alton 62
D'Arcy 24, 26, 61, 101, 114, 118
  Revd John 54, 55, 56, 57, 58, 59, 60, 61, 62, 63, 64, 65, 66, 67, 68, 69, 70, 72, 74, 75, 80, 81, 82, 83, 85, 87, 90, 94, 95, 96, 97, 99, 101, 103, 104, 105, 107, 108, 109, 110, 111, 112, 113, 114, 115, 117, 118, 119
Dale 80
Dalton 62, 101, 107
Daly 26, 100
  Revd James .. 44, 48, 49, 50, 51, 52, 53, 54, 55, 56, 57, 58, 59, 60, 61, 62, 63, 64, 65, 66, 67, 68, 69, 70, 71, 72, 73, 74, 75, 77, 78, 79, 81, 82, 83, 85, 86, 87, 88, 89, 91, 92, 93, 95, 103, 104, 105, 110, 111, 115,

117, 118, 119, 120, 121, 122, 123, 140, 142
Daniel 44, 58
Darcy 60, 61, 139
Darne 83
Darnel 103, 113
Darnell 103
Davey 106
Davidson 24, 91
Davies 32, 64, 106
Davin 26
Davis 28, 33, 51, 56, 74, 81, 102, 107, 112, 131, 138
Day 82, 127
Deace 65
Deacers 114
Deacon 85
Deal 38
Deane 25, 26
Debutts 27
Delano 27
Delmage 115
Denis 69, 70
Dennis 49, 54, 63, 75, 77, 91
Dennison 98
Dennisson 80, 110
Derinzey 29
Develin 26
Devenish 33, 34, 37, 39, 42, 44, 47, 56, 74, 133, 135, 138
Devereux 26, 130
Dickinson 51, 57, 63
Digby 33
Dignan 69
Dillon 34, 55
Divine 91
Dix 54, 58
Do 67
Dobbin 79
Dodgeworth 110, 128
Dodgworth 35
Dodsworth 56
Doe 62
Dolan 27, 76
Donahoe 90, 96, 98
Donahue 92
Donaldson 107
Donnelly 75
Donoghue 30
Donovan 28, 31
Doolan 117
Douglass 117
Dow 65, 88
Doyle 24, 66, 69, 111
Driscoll 58

156

Driver	25
Duane	74
Duff	106
Duffy	52
Duncan	49, 77, 104
Dunleavy	50
Dunn	24
Dwyer	54, 71
Dyas	72
Dyer	48
Eames	55
Eaton	26, 128
Eddington	29, 37, 46
Edington	50, 56
Edmunds	70
Edwards	125
Efford	99
Egan	37, 81
Elliott	113
Evans	31, 39, 109
Eyre	24, 43, 92
Fahey	92
Fairclough	102
Fallon	96
Farrel	63
Farrell	139
Farrington	33, 37, 40, 43, 46, 57, 134, 138
Fayne	91
Ferg	74
Ferguson	122
Ferris	133
ffrench	64
Ffrench	73, 83, 85, 125
Field	24, 36
Fields	126
Fife	109
Filtus	83
Fineran	51
Firth	51
Fisher	56
Fitzgerald	50
FitzGibbon	129
Fitzimmons	61
Fitzimons	46
FitzPatrick	25, 29, 50, 61, 86
Fitzsimons	54, 61, 88, 102, 104
Flahertie	141
Flanagan	31, 82
Flanigan	86
Flannery	26, 55, 62
Flury	70
Flyn	26
Flynn	98
Fochead	142
Foley	52, 54, 56, 68, 78, 87, 92, 110
Foran	113
Forbes	47, 65, 125, 131, 139
Ford	55, 64
Forsayeth	91
Forster	51, 61, 92, 103, 121
Foster	113
Fowler	69
Fox	73
Foy	65
Frances	41
Francis	37, 133, 137
Franklin	69
Fraser	91
Frazer	81
Frean	29
Freeland	74
Freeman	123, 124
French	38, 48, 64, 107
Frith	56, 57, 58
Fry	49, 110, 119
Fullick	99
Furlong	87, 91, 141
Furry	71
Fynn	88, 89
Fyrrall	69
Gain	28
Galagher	44
Gallagher	79
Gamble	84
Gannon	81
Gardiner	105, 141
Garret	58
Garrette	55
Gaskins	43
Gavin	66, 116
Geherty	55
Geoghehan	63
George	97
Geraghty	58, 64
Gibbons	36, 84, 124
Gibson	32
Gilchrist	88
Giles	30, 77
Gill	55, 76, 140
Given	40
Glanville	76
Glennan	79, 83
Glyn	92, 131
Glynn	55, 62, 79, 84, 92, 102, 122, 123, 124, 125
Goddard	99
Goggin	33
Goldtrip	31
Goodfellow	45
Goodman	49

Goodwin	113
Graghane	65
Graham	56, 100
Grainger	96, 98, 102, 103, 111
Gramsden	111
Grandy	34, 134
Granger	112
Grant	132
Graves	41
Gray	35, 96
Green	43, 71, 133
Greham	109, 110
Grehan	95
Greuber	115
Grey	58, 69
Griffin	62, 118
Griffith	28, 37, 39, 41, 42, 45, 110, 138
Griffiths	33, 46
Grogan	98
Groom	35
Groonet	52
Guest	67
Gunberton	119
Gunning	66
Gunton	48
Guthrie	134
Hacker	48
Hacket	52
Hair	109
Haliday	102
Halliday	139
Halloran	53
Hamilton	36, 45, 53, 83, 105
Hanbury	26
Handcock	28, 70, 108
Hanna	25
Hannon	96
Harbeson	108
Hare	55, 83, 95
Harms	42, 45, 140
Harris	40, 81
Harrison	57, 80, 95
Hart	25, 49, 92, 135
Hasler	96
Hay	76
Hazlette	100
Healy	117, 142
Hearn	38, 139, 140
Hearnan	70
Heavy	40, 42, 57
Hedger	25
Hedrington	24
Henigan	53
Henry	109, 127
Hensley	125
Herbert	96
Herdman	27
Hickey	31
Hickie	67
Hicks	26
Higgins	65, 70, 71, 79
Hill	105, 132
Hills	33, 132
Hinks	126
Hobard	81
Hockland	93
Hodgens	31
Hodgins	140
Hodson	52
Hogan	93, 120
Holland	52
Holleran	43, 52
Holles	93
Holliday	24
Hollis	89
Holly	44
Hollywood	29
Hopkins	56, 61, 75
Horan	31
Horsefall	24
Hoskins	114
How	62
Howard	64, 86
Hubbart	39
Hubbert	42, 46
Hubbett	40
Hudley	75
Hudson	128
Huggard	28
Hughe	43
Hughes	40, 46, 61, 101, 131, 132, 137, 140
Humphreys	141
Hunter	106, 107, 137
Huse	94
Huston	68
Hutchinson	29, 43, 66, 68, 127
Hynes	79
Iggs	84
Ingle	101
Ingram	112
Irvine	87, 133
Irwin	59, 77
Ives	96
Jackson	33, 50, 67, 85, 132
James	43, 97, 98
Jannes	133
Janns	32
Jaques	24
Jeffers	34
Johns	74, 107

Johnson 27, 72, 82, 105, 132
Johnston 86, 90, 118
Johnstone 75
Joll 94
Jolly 125, 128
Jones 24, 35, 132
Jordan 114
Jorible 105
Joy 44
Joyce 60, 143
Joyes 25
Joynt 44, 63
Kavars 66
Kealy 62, 117
Keane 28
Kearney 76, 79, 82, 85, 86, 105, 126
Keating 110
Keatinge 65
Keevers 142
Kelly 25, 26, 29, 32, 35, 51, 57, 64, 81, 94, 111, 113, 142
Kennedy 27, 30, 47, 50
Kenny 43, 45, 56, 63, 70, 77, 86, 113
Keogh 71
Kerr 83, 105
Kiggins 26
Kilkelly 93
Killeny 91
Killery 73, 95, 111
Kilroy 50, 55
Kimmoth 68
Kine 34, 134
King 43, 52, 67, 71
Kirby 62, 131
Kirwan 27, 28, 30, 117, 121, 122, 123
Knee 94
Knight 30, 85, 90
Knowles 33, 137
Lackey 26, 35, 37, 39, 45, 71, 124, 132, 138
Lacy 102, 122
Laing 111, 119
Lally 52, 72
Lambert .. 82, 106, 108, 112, 115, 116, 120
Langly 54
Larkin 73
Larklin 69
Latty 38
Laurence 56, 68, 75
Law 117
Lawrence 44, 50, 87
Lawton 29
Leath 76
Leckey 135, 136
Lee 34

Leech 31
Leeson 40
Lenaghan 48
Lennen 40
Leonard 48, 84
Leslie 29, 130
Lewin 24
Lewis 39, 133, 139
Little 104
Littlefield 89, 90, 120
Lodge 111
Loftus 57
Logan 69, 142
Logun 64
Loney 39
Looker 116
Lord 142
Love 98
Loxton 93
Lydon 56, 109, 126
Lynch 24, 26, 30, 31, 35, 44, 46, 47, 48, 53, 60, 61, 85, 131
Lyons 58, 115, 133
Lyster 35
Macartey 97
Macarthy 39, 43, 63
Macartney 51, 130, 140
Macarty 33
MacCleary 97
MacDannel 55
MacDonald 101
MacDorig 140
Machanally 33
Mackay 32
Mackenzie 130
Mackey 130
Macklin 102
Mackye 103
Macleery 83
MacMahon 79, 104
Macnamara 49
Macqueen 31
Maculla 137
Macullogh 130, 131, 136
Madden 58
Madigan 58
Magan 33
Mahon 31, 60, 64, 66, 73, 80, 86
Maleod 130
Malim 26
Malley 26, 94
Mandie 58
Manhal 140
Manion 52
Mannen 24, 63

Mannin 53
Manning 42, 44, 60, 86, 97, 98, 99, 101,
  102, 104, 105, 106, 107, 108, 109, 111,
  112, 115, 116, 117, 118, 119, 120
Mannion 54, 66, 87
Marget 52
Marlow 57
Marshal.. 39, 133
Marshall...................................... 61, 96, 129
Martin 24, 25, 31, 35, 36, 51, 61, 67, 68,
  84, 87, 104, 105, 106, 110
Martyn 65, 92
Mason 35, 36, 38, 39, 42, 46, 113, 125,
  139, 140
Massy 70
Mathews 41
Maunsell 54, 79, 89, 142
  Revd Edward Eyre ... 79, 80, 94, 98, 99,
    100, 101, 102, 103, 104, 106, 107,
    108, 110, 111, 112, 113, 114, 115,
    116, 118, 119, 125, 126, 127
Maxwell. 65, 66, 72, 73, 77, 78, 79, 82, 83,
  91, 103, 123, 131, 133
Mc Solde 86
Mcana 56
McArthy 39
McCabe 25
McCane 51
McCarrol 40, 41, 43, 123
McCarroll 123
McCarthy 60
McCartney 92
McCarty 72
McCleery 85
McColough.. 46
McConnell...................................... 46, 99
McCulla 50
McCullogh...................................... 36, 52
McCully 41
McDannel.. 122
McDermot 81, 87, 91
McDermott 102, 112
McDonal... 94
McDonald................................. 26, 27, 57
McDonnell..................................... 50, 79
McDonogh................. 38, 44, 47, 116, 118
McDonough .. 59, 64, 68, 87, 95, 102, 123,
  124
McEntire 109
McGanley 71
McGowan 82
McGrath 63, 112, 115
McGregor 78, 129
McIntosh 137
McLachlan.. 78

McLean.. 114, 136
McLinn 122
McLoughlin..................................... 75, 83
McMahon 112
McNab 97
McNabb 34
McNally 112
McNamara 115
McNeice 83
McPherson 44
McPhirls 118
McWalter.. 108
Meartis 132
Mellain 66
Mellet... 27
Melville 94
Merchant.. 69
Middleton 58, 67, 127
Millmay 47
Mills... 55
Milway 140
Minchin 88
Minehan... 104
Mitchel 55
Mitchell 74, 89, 124
Mitchelle.. 71
Mittchell 89
Moffet.. 47
Molowny 69
Monad.. 117
Monaghan 36, 68, 141
Montgomery 49
Moody 137
Moore 51, 53, 66, 134, 136
Moran 63, 84, 87, 91, 136, 140, 142
Morgan 31, 32, 64, 74, 76, 78, 99, 106, 119
  Revd Henry .. 53, 54, 55, 56, 57, 58, 59,
    60, 61, 62, 63, 64, 65, 66, 68, 69,
    70, 71, 72, 73, 74, 75, 76, 77, 78,
    79, 80, 81, 82, 83, 84, 85, 86, 89,
    90, 91, 93, 94, 95, 96, 97, 98, 99,
    100, 101, 102, 103, 104, 105, 106,
    107, 108, 109, 110, 111, 112, 113,
    114, 115, 116, 117, 118, 119, 120,
    124, 125, 126, 127, 141, 142
Morphet 54
Morris 103, 109, 115
Morrison 130
Mortimer........ 28, 34, 37, 39, 46, 49, 57, 61
Mulhall 133
Mulholland 138
Mulin 75
Mullen 48, 104, 118
Mullin 103
Mullins 55, 70

Mulvany 111
Munroe 91
Murphy 35, 42, 51, 79, 103, 108, 126, 127, 131, 134
Murray 65, 68, 84
Murry 76
Myers.. 113
Mylan 32
Naghten 26
Neil 108
Neligan 33
Nesbett... 113
Nethercoot... 99
Neville 101, 102
Newel 50
Nicolson 131
Nislor... 58
Nolan 50, 54, 135
Norman.............................. 32, 102, 122
North 79
Nowlan 87
O Donnell 50
O Flaherty...................................... 24, 50
O Laughlin 25
O'Brian.. 33
O'Brien 27, 37, 41, 42, 43, 45, 48, 50, 53, 60, 63, 80, 82, 84, 85, 94, 100, 104, 113, 136, 138
O'Callaghan 51
O'Connell....................................... 35, 36
O'Connor...................................... 115, 136
O'Donnell.............................. 35, 89, 120
O'Flaherty 86, 89
O'Hara............................... 54, 67, 89
O'Loughlin 33
O'Maly 107
O'Neil 88
O'Neill... 38
O'Shaughnessy..................................... 43
O'Sullivan 62
O'Toole 51
Oakes 64, 67, 87
Ormsby .51, 52, 53, 54, 59, 71, 88, 92, 103
Painter 112
Pard... 62
Parke... 115
Parker 24, 38, 49, 59, 74, 88, 90
Parry 108, 142
Pasley 29
Patterson 98
Pear.. 37, 130, 138
Peare 42, 45, 49, 51, 62
Pears 132, 135, 140
Perry 70, 82
Persse.......... 38, 71, 85, 104, 108, 113, 117

Peshill 36
Peters 64
Phillips... 25, 40
Phirls... 118
Piew 123
Pigott 53
Pipper.. 77
Platt... 61
Plunket.. 108
Plunketh.. 94
Plunkett... 108
Pope 84
Poppleton...................................... 68, 110
Porter 84
Potter 77, 80, 88, 90, 93
Pottle... 111
Powel 59, 81
Power 54
Pratt 100
Prendergast 67, 81
Preston 43
Price 119
Prido 52
Pritchard 95
Prosser 44, 77
Pue 103
Pugh..................... 36, 122, 123, 132, 134
Purdie.. 24, 29
Quigley 82, 99, 103, 107, 122
Quigly 82, 103, 123, 124
Quin 92, 105
Rachars 58
Raine... 51
Ram 50
Ramage 48
Ramsay 103, 123
Rankin 62
Rea 111
Redfern 96
Reed............. 47, 62, 85, 92, 116, 121, 122
Reeley 63
Regan 53, 97
Reid 85, 96, 104, 115
Reilly 56, 64, 65, 68, 70, 74, 88, 89, 92, 114, 123, 124
Reily 30, 122
Renfry 114
Richardson....31, 40, 77, 83, 106, 111, 114
Rielly 101
Righton 50
Rimminton.. 102
Rippingham 51
Roberts 50, 52, 122, 123, 124, 128, 135
Robertson 78

161

Robinson 27, 33, 38, 39, 40, 46, 54, 57, 70, 132, 135, 136, 137, 139
Robson 125
Rogers 53
Roland 111
Rollin 64
Rooney 74
Roony 54
Royse 85
Rubens 30
Rud 50, 52, 103
Rush 106, 114
Rutherford 35
Ruxton 77, 83, 88, 99
Ryan 33, 52, 58, 64, 69, 87, 110, 140
Sadlier 56
Salkeld 99
Salters 104
Sampson 107
Satliffe 65
Saver 58
Scanlan 73
Schahill 87
Scorry 52
Scot 111
Scott. 31, 36, 37, 38, 39, 42, 44, 50, 84, 96, 132, 134, 137, 138, 140
Seagrave 30
Seaman 102
Seeds 51
Sergeant 30
Sewell 49
Sexton 53, 102
Shannen 71
Sharp 102
Shaughnessy 48, 102, 123
Shaughnesy 123
Shaugnessy 122
Shaw 36, 40, 41, 45, 49, 60, 100, 122, 128, 139
    Revd Robert . 24, 30, 41, 128, 129, 141, 143
Shawe 38, 41
Shea 101
Shedrake 57
Shepherd 25
Sheppard 60
Sheridan 25
Sherwood 49
Shields 32
Shildrick 86
Shone 50, 90
Short 33
Shuffell 33
Simcockes 41, 42, 43, 45, 46, 133, 135

Simmonds 63
Simpson 45, 76, 86, 91, 131, 136
Singleton 98
Skerrett 34
Slammion 34
Slater 51, 86
Slow 81, 114
Smith 36, 37, 44, 47, 53, 63, 68, 77, 90, 109, 110, 117, 120, 123, 132, 137
Smyth..... 28, 34, 38, 39, 50, 51, 65, 73, 79, 81, 95, 102, 122, 123, 124, 131, 135, 140
Sockel 112
Spelman 85, 116, 120
Spright 93
Squibb 27, 128, 130, 132
Standford 24
Stanley 86
Staunton 30
Steadman 49, 50, 51, 52, 53, 54, 55, 56, 57, 58, 59, 60, 62, 64, 65, 66, 67, 68, 69, 70, 71, 72, 74, 78, 79, 81, 82, 83, 84, 85, 86, 87, 90, 91, 92, 93, 94, 141, 142
Steden 108
Stedman 128, 141
Stephens 48, 64, 66, 67, 80, 82, 90, 91, 97, 109, 112, 114
Sterling 134
Stewart 34, 55, 91, 114
Stirling 34
Stoakes 89
Stocker 96
Stone 88
Storey 39, 41, 44, 47, 140
Strachan 65
Stratron 83
Strogen 125, 141
Stuart 98, 102
Suffield 47
Sullivan 86, 91
Sutherland 63
Swan 51, 59, 78, 86, 99, 102
Sweehins 96
Sweeney 55
Sweny 30, 56
Swords 56
Symmers 49, 56, 74
Symmond 67
Symons 116
Taffe 58
Taffy 112
Taggart 34, 38, 41, 43, 46, 102, 134
Talmedge 95
Tarleton 87

Taylor 35, 63, 64, 101, 128
Telford 85
Tellford 113
Tennant 31, 37, 130, 132, 135, 139
Thomas .. 24, 29, 30, 31, 32, 39, 42, 45, 56, 81, 112, 128, 131, 133
Thompson 30, 57, 68, 94, 128
Threlford 97
Tiernan 49
Tierney 26, 92
Tighe 47
Timms 34
Tirrel 52
Toole 90
Tooring 87
Topham 65, 68
Tounsille 84
Townsend 54
Tracy 53, 74
Travis 97
Trelford 107
Trench 92
Trimble 74
Trins 60
Trounsell 108, 109
Trumble 34
Turner 34
Tvey 24
Tweedy 25
Tyrrell 28
Upfield 73
Vinicombe 32
Vining 108
von Hardenburg 54
Vordun 72
Wade 36
Wakefield 49
Walker 35, 133
Wallace 94, 143
Walsh. 27, 32, 43, 46, 60, 83, 89, 129, 132, 138
Ward 32, 94, 125
Wardsworth 33
Ware 97
Warren 34, 52
Waters 49, 55, 107
Waterson 77
Watts 48
Webb 82, 103, 109, 117
Welby 109
Wells 93
Welsh 135
West 55

Wheeler . 25, 34, 35, 37, 40, 42, 46, 48, 52, 54, 56, 61, 65, 66, 72, 77, 81, 86, 95, 107, 116, 138, 139
Whelan 65, 87
Whelnal 128
Whistler 104, 113, 133
White 66, 98, 101, 104, 127
Whiteheir 40
Whitestone 30
Whitley 99, 100
  Revd John 51, 52, 53, 54, 56, 57, 58, 60, 61, 62, 63, 65, 66, 67, 68, 69, 70, 72, 75, 76, 77, 78, 81, 83, 84, 87, 88, 89, 90, 91, 92, 93, 94, 95, 96, 97, 99, 100, 101, 104, 110, 111, 113, 115, 117, 118, 119, 141, 142
Wiggen 42
Wigger 136
Wild 102
Wilde 122, 126
Wilkins 41, 42, 46, 102
Williams 55, 62, 63, 103, 122, 123, 124
Williamson 113
Willian 138
Wilson 47, 52, 62, 87, 116
Wilton 61, 66, 75, 89
Winnett 120
Winter 37
Woods 88
Woolner 73
Wray 26
Wright 75, 108, 113, 142
Wyld 123
Wylde 123
Wylie 92
Wynn 98, 116
Wynter 29
Yardley 99
Yellon 62
Young 109, 138
Younge 36, 37